D1281005

# ARISTOTLE IN THE WEST

## WORKS BY THE SAME AUTHOR

*Siger de Brabant d'après ses œuvres inédites.* Two vol. (Les Philosophes Belges, XII-XIII). Louvain, 1931-1942; XVI-760 p. (Out of print).

*Les œuvres et la doctrine de Siger de Brabant.* (Mémoire couronné par l'Académie Royale de Belgique). Brussels, 1938; 196 p.

*Aristote en Occident. Les origines de l'aristotélisme parisien.* Louvain, 1946; 200 p. (Out of print).

*Directives pour la confection d'une monographie scientifique.* Third ed. Louvain, 1961; 90 p.

*Epistemology.* New York, 1949; XIV-324 p. (Also French, Italian, German, Spanish, Chinese and Dutch editions). New English ed. Louvain-New York, 1970.

*Ontology.* New York, 1952; 280 p. (Also French, Italian, Spanish and German editions). New English ed. Louvain-New York, 1970.

*Philosophie des Mittelalters.* (Bibliographische Einführungen in das Studium der Philosophie, 17). Bern, 1950; 52 p.

*Le XIII<sup>e</sup> siècle.* In A. Forest, F. Van Steenberghen, M. de Gandillac, *Le mouvement doctrinal du IX<sup>e</sup> et XIV<sup>e</sup> siècle.* (Histoire de l'Église depuis les origines jusqu'à nos jours, vol. 13). Paris, 2d ed. 1956; p. 191-348.

*The Philosophical Movement in the Thirteenth Century.* (Belfast Lectures 1953). Edinburgh, 1955; X-116 p.

*Histoire de la philosophie.* Période chrétienne. Louvain, 1964; 196 p. Spanish and Polish editions.

*Hidden God. How do we know that God exists?* Louvain-Saint Louis, 1966; 316 p. (Also French, German, Italian, Spanish and Portuguese editions).

*La philosophie au XIII<sup>e</sup> siècle.* (Philosophes médiévaux, IX). Louvain, 1966; 594 p.

*Le retour à saint Thomas a-t-il encore un sens aujourd'hui?* (Conférence Albert-le-Grand 1967). Montreal-Paris, 1967; 62 p.

IMPRIMATUR

Lovanii, die 7<sup>a</sup> Octobris 1954.

H. VAN WAEYENBERGH,
Rect. Univers., deleg.

# ARISTOTLE IN THE WEST

*The Origins of*
*Latin Aristotelianism*

BY

FERNAND VAN STEENBERGHEN
PROFESSOR AT THE UNIVERSITY OF LOUVAIN

TRANSLATED BY

LEONARD JOHNSTON
PROFESSOR AT USHAW COLLEGE, DURHAM

SECOND EDITION

NAUWELAERTS PUBLISHING HOUSE
LOUVAIN (BELGIUM)
1970

© 1970 by Editions Nauwelaerts

All rights of adaptation and reprinting including microfilms
reserved to all countries.

# CONTENTS

189
St 32 à 2

# PREFACE

After a long period of neglect and even of contempt, medieval philosophy is now attracting an increasingly sympathetic attention. This philosophy reached its apogee in the thirteenth century; and historians agree in recognising that the penetration of Aristotelianism was the decisive factor in its rapid development. The main object of this book is to show how the union between Aristotelianism and traditional Christian thought came about.

There is, however, another point of interest in this enquiry. Many people today are turning to Thomas Aquinas in their search for the basis of a solid and living philosophy. Now, in spite of the improvement in medieval studies, many disciples of Aquinas still treat Thomism as if it were timeless, and interpret it without taking sufficient account of the historical environment in which it came to birth. This lack of historical perspective is prejudicial to the understanding of the authentic thought of the master; the exact point and precise meaning may be obscured; one may fail to distinguish St. Thomas's own views from those he merely borrows from his environment; one may confuse his key ideas with those he adopts merely through pressure of events or through the exigencies of controversies of the moment.

The following pages may be looked on as a contribution to the study of the historical origins of Thomism. For the most part, they are taken from a scientific monograph devoted to Siger of Brabant, the Parisian master contemporary with Thomas Aquinas[1]. Chapter II of that work (pp. 357-497) dealt with *Philosophy at the University of Paris before Siger of Brabant*; and indulgent critics thought that this enquiry into the origins of medieval Aristotelianism might interest a wider audience than that aimed at by the collection *Les Philosophes Belges*. Most of the notes have been omitted, as well as certain elaborations which were intended rather for specialists. The reader anxious for more complete documentation will find in the original any fuller information and references he may desire.

The French edition of this essay appeared in 1946 and has long been out of print. The English edition presented here is not just a translation of the French edition. It has been brought up to date in the light of recent publications, and three new chapters have been added: one on the origins of Aristotelianism at Oxford, another on the career of Siger of Brabant, and a third on the great condemnation of Aristotelianism in 1277. These additions are taken mainly from the study of the thirteenth century published by me in *Histoire de l'Église depuis les Origines jusqu'à nos jours*[2].

[1] F. VAN STEENBERGHEN, *Siger de Brabant d'après ses œuvres inédites* (Les Philosophes Belges, t. XII et XIII). Two vols. in 4°, pp. xvi-760. Louvain, Éditions de l'Institut supérieur de Philosophie, 1931-1942.

[2] Volume 13. *Le Mouvement doctrinal du IXe au XIVe siècle* by A. FOREST, F. VAN STEENBERGHEN, M. DE GANDILLAC. One vol. in-8, 480 pp., Paris, Bloud and Gay, 1951. See pp. 177-328.

I have not mentioned in this book the reaction to my interpretation of the philosophical movement in the thirteenth century, because I have dealt with it in my *Belfast Lectures* of 1953, which are to be published shortly. This work will also give useful material complementary to the present study.

The history of western thought in the thirteenth century is dominated by an event of incalculable importance: Christian thought, still young and growing, made its first serious contact and first large-scale fusion with the fruits of pagan thought (Greek and Arabian). Before we study the history of this important event, we must first rapidly describe the two cultural trends concerned in the encounter. That is the object of the first two chapters; they will give a brief account of the historical antecedents of thirteenth century thought. Then we shall try to sketch the main stages of the philosophical movement in the first seventy years of the thirteenth century, taking as concrete cases the universities of Paris and Oxford. In these universities one can see the gradual development of Latin Aristotelianism, and the first philosophical syntheses to which it gave rise.

This translation is due to Fr. L. JOHNSTON, professor at Ushaw College, Durham; and grateful acknowledgement is due to Fr. Bernard PAYNE, librarian at the same College, who read the manuscript and made useful suggestions.

Louvain, February 2nd, 1954.

# CHAPTER I

# THE GREEK AND ARABIAN SYNTHESES

There is something subjective and arbitrary in every system constructed by the mind of man; but two enduring factors limit this arbitrary character of the mind's endeavor to depict and express reality: the nature of the objects to be known, and that of the knowing subject. Thus, the history of thought reveals many points of agreement among philosophical systems and religious conceptions, in spite of their diversity. This enables us to classify them, showing how they are all based on a few dominant viewpoints and typical attitudes.

The truth of this statement becomes evident when we try to work out the general results of the scientific and philosophical progress achieved by the Greeks within that civilization, first Hellenic, then Hellenistic, which is at the origin of all the later civilizations of Europe, Western Asia and North Africa. We meet first of all with a fundamental duality, that of rational thought and religious beliefs (in the widest sense of the expression). We find men trying to solve by their own efforts the mystery of the universe; but in so far as this mystery is beyond them, they are only too glad to seek enlightenment from higher "revelation", which they hoped would give them access to a new knowledge, divine in origin. With the Greeks, scientific thought goes side by side with popular beliefs, first of all mythology, and then, in the Hellenistic period, mystery religions imported from the east. This parallel advance scarcely ever provokes clashes or conflicts, for it is only in neo-Platonism that religion and philosophy come into really close contact. In the rational or philosophical sphere, Greek thought oscillates between the two poles of Idealism and Empiricism, which are henceforward to be found at all stages of history, and which are personified by the two greatest geniuses of antiquity, Plato and Aristotle. It is from the complex nature of our consciousness that this antithesis results. One moment we try to imitate the mode of thought of pure intelligences and seek the secret of reality in its first principle; at another we tend rather to resort to the tangible data of observation or sensible experience.

Plato, and after him the neo-Platonists, stand for *ancient idealism*; that is, a system of thought directed towards the spiritual world of Ideas, thought which seeks to raise itself above our human status in order to communicate, as far as possible, with divine thought. Platonism, and still more neo-Platonism, are thus essentially metaphysical doctrines, as well as being doctrines admitting of religious feeling and mystical contemplation. These systems call for an ethic of detachment and spiritual progress, aiming at something superior to anything the world can offer—the life of beatific communication with God. The Middle Ages would have direct knowledge of Platonism and neo-Platonism only through three dialogues of Plato and a few writings of Proclus. But the influence of these philosophies became really important through numerous indirect infiltrations.

The main elements in the Platonic tradition are these:

—the *intuition of Ideas* or intelligibles and in general the possibility of direct knowledge of the spiritual world and the Supreme Being;

—the affirmation of a reality which transcends absolutely the world of our sensible experience and which is the first source of every reality, namely the *Good* (in Plato's system), or the *One* (in the systems of Plotinus and Proclus);

—the doctrine of *participation*, which sees those beings which are distinct from the Supreme Being as derivative, dependent realities, whose ontological value results from the degree to which they "participate" in the perfection of the first principle; from this is derived the *hierarchical* conception of the universe and the theory of *emanation*, which are meant to explain the process of divine causality;

—the conception of *matter* as non-being, as multiplicity, as principle of evil;

—*psychological dualism*, which juxtaposes and even opposes the soul and body, treating them as antagonistic substances;

—lastly, the idea of liberation from matter and the *return to God* through asceticism and contemplation.

Aristotle, on the contrary, represents *scientific empiricism*. In reacting against Plato's doctrine of Ideas, he worked out a philosophical system which claims to be based on nothing but the observation of cosmic realities and the data of consciousness. His *theory of knowledge* and his penetrating analyses of the processes of discursive thought made him the founder of science and the creator of logic. His treatises on *natural philosophy* offer an ingenious and very coherent interpretation of all phenomena which go to make up our material universe. Those on *ethics*, bearing the stamp of the same empirical method, are full of valuable analyses of the life of the individual and of society in general. They set forth rules of conduct which have rational judgment for their inspiration. But, as we might expect, Aristotle's weak point is his *metaphysics*. As a physicist, a naturalist, a sociologist, he is without peer, but not so as a metaphysician. We must however be careful not to carry this judgment too far. Aristotle is the founder of metaphysical *science*. His books on "first philosophy" bring a remarkable effort of analysis to bear on the fundamental metaphysical concepts and already indicate a great development in the working out of several metaphysical doctrines, concerning truth, causes, substance, unity, matter and form and the like. We also find him attempting a metaphysical synthesis, using the idea of analogy, the conception of the hierarchy of causes and the affirmation of the existence of spiritual substances, at whose summit is enthroned the First Mover or Pure Act. But viewing them, as we are now able to do, in their proper perspective, we can see how deficient this metaphysical synthesis and this "theology" are, in that they leave the fundamental problems of ontology unsolved.

For Aristotle, the First Mover is the final cause of cosmic evolution, but it does not seem to move the world as an efficient cause of movement. Certainly it is not a cause of being or a creative cause. We ought therefore to think of the hierarchy of spiritual substances and that of material species as realities both necessary and eternal. This absolute is thus multiple, ordered and changing, thereby giving rise to metaphysical problems which Aristotle does not even consider. For example:

—the eternity of the world, of movement and of time seems to him a necessary postulate which he does not seek to justify on the metaphysical plane;

—he does not try to find the ultimate reason for the order of the universe, but sees it as a fact, an object of observation;

—in his system, explanation is fairly similar to scientific explanation as we understand it nowadays— given a series of facts, and without trying to determine their ultimate source or their deepest nature, how must we enunciate the laws governing the evolution of that series ?

Aristotle's metaphysics, like all systems before neo-Platonism, is incomplete and unfinished, and those problems which it does raise are too superficial and cover too narrow a field. Supposing we had to consider Aristotle's system as definitive, as an explanation of the real which claimed to be exhaustive, we should be obliged to see it as an ill-defined form of cosmic pantheism. For within the system the spiritual substances and the material world are in possession of the fundamental attributes of the absolute, namely an existence which is eternal and necessary. Let us, however, give Aristotle the benefit of the doubt with regard to the points on which he is silent. It will suffice to say that he did not deal with the essential problem of metaphysics, that of existence.

At all events, there could be no question of finding in this philosophy, as some have tried to do, a true *theism* and still less a "rigorous theism". If Aristotle's First Mover or Pure Act is a personal being, even the most perfect personal being, it is still neither a creative cause nor providence, and its transcendence, in comparison with the other immaterial substances, is altogether relative.

The gaps in Aristotle's metaphysics cannot but cause enormous difficulties in the field of *human psychology*. We must remember, if we are to understand it, that the problem of our own nature is perhaps the most difficult of philosophical problems. Man, the point at which the spiritual and material universes meet, is a microcosm, and the strange complexity of his nature is the first source of our difficulty. What in us is "matter" and what "spirit"? How are these two principles united, and in what way do they combine to produce our complete human activity? The difficulties become profoundly mysterious when we broach the problem of the origin of the spiritual soul. Here, Aristotle was probably out of his depth, for his metaphysics would offer no possible solution, without detriment to those psychological data which he doubtless prized above all else, in accordance with his normal method. In fact, as our own consciousness testifies, intellectual activity is an activity of the living substance of which man consists. For Aristotle, thought is even the specific difference which makes an animal a human being, a transitory being which is born, which develops and which disappears in death. On the other hand, this intellectual activity, the importance of which is admirably emphasized in the treatises of the *Organon*, shows itself to be an immaterial, impassible reality, transcending corporeal things and separated from matter. Thus, the intellect belongs to the world of the eternal, the incorruptible, the divine. The wisdom of Aristotle goes no further than this. At the birth of an individual, where does the intellect that makes him capable of thought come from? How is it united to the other parts of the soul? If it existed before the individual, in what world did it live, what part did it play in that world, why does it now unite itself to a human body? What becomes of the intellect after the death of the individual? Aristotle asks himself hardly any of these questions; to none of them does he give an answer. His disciples tried to solve them in different ways, but not one of them succeeded in doing so, without betraying in some important particular the teaching of the master. Alexander of Aphrodisias sacrificed the immaterial character of the intellect; Averroes destroyed the personality of the human individual; Thomas Aquinas preserved both these things, but his teaching on the origin of the human soul is altogether foreign to the system of Aristotle. A spiritual soul can begin its existence at the moment when a new human organism is constituted, that is, at the end of a biological process accomplished in time. This same spiritual soul, owing to its truly connatural relationship with the organism, can subsist as the principle of determination and of life for the human being thus called into existence. In order to understand all this, one needs to possess a very exact notion of the act of creation, and to realize that in the permanent influx of the creative Cause lies the ultimate reason of the existence, the continuation and the evolution of all substances constituting the created order. Of this notion Aristotle is altogether ignorant. We must praise Aristotle for his reserve in the face of these formidable problems, but we should also realize that his human psychology is extremely disappointing, all the more because these uncertainties on the subject of the intellect entail an agnosticism which is even more disappointing with respect to the future life and final destiny of man.

The influence of Aristotle's work was immense and, as Father Mandonnet points out, the reason for this success was inherent in the nature, the method and the value of his work. In fact, the scientific work of Aristotle, taken as a whole, represents the most solid and most extensive result of Greek intellectual activity. Before Aristotle, there had been the developments of the old naturalist and idealist schools, and the Eleatics had invented the dialectical method. He himself had witnessed the new direction given to philosophy by Socrates and Plato. Having selected all the fruitful elements of this tradition, he was able on his own initiative to develop and systematize them with that rigorous method which has become synonymous with his name and genius. His development of science and philosophy, in so far as Hellenic society was capable of producing them, was as wide and profound as it could be. He summarizes and brings to a close a race's intellectual effort; his writings are the fruits of an entire civilization (and we should not forget that no ancient people could equal the Greeks in the art of research or in the gift for intellectual discovery). The work of Aristotle therefore, being so vast an encyclopaedia of ancient knowledge, was as it were a reserve of energy, an intellectual capital, to be transmitted during the course of the centuries to races and societies of men. And these men, finding it in their path, would desire to be born into the life of thought. So it was that Aristotle became the pedagogue of four or five civilizations—the Alexandrine Greeks, the Syrians, the Arabs, and the Jews of the time of Maimonides, while what we now call modern

Europe has been more influenced by him than any other society.

However, the spread of Aristotelianism was not to go unopposed, nor would it fail to stir up great controversies. The tendency towards empiricism and agnosticism exhibited by Aristotle was destined to arouse the distrust of the religiously minded and would not satisfy metaphysicians; the gaps and obscurities in his system were to give ground for endless discussions among his disciples. Almost always, thinkers who have found their inspiration in the peripatetic philosophy have found themselves bound to correct or complete the views of the Stagirite with ideas borrowed from Platonism and neo-Platonism.

The Arab conquest, in the seventh century of the Christian era, was the starting-point for a new civilization in the southern basin of the Mediterranean. Mingling with the peoples they subdued, the Arabs showed an extraordinary power of assimilation; their culture had nothing really original about it, even in religion; but they were able to reap great benefit from the hellenistic civilization. In philosophy, together with the Jews who inhabited their empire, they exploited the treasures of Greek thought. Thus continued the movement which was to bring the legacy of Greek knowledge to the Latin West, by the roundabout way of Syria, Egypt, Mauretania and Spain, until the crusades made direct intellectual relations with the Eastern Empire possible.

The term "Arabianism" can be used to designate all philosophical trends which developed in the countries conquered by the Arabs. In this development Moslems and Jews played parallel parts.

In both Moslem and Jewish worlds, a profoundly religious civilization provided a background for philosophical development, and philosophers, much more than the Greek thinkers, had to take account of the existence of a religion having as its marks revelation, authority and orthodoxy. Such a situation, almost entirely unknown to the Greeks and Romans, brought some new factors to the fore, such as the reciprocal influences of rational thought and religious beliefs, doctrinal conflicts, a search for a balance between rival doctrines, or for a conciliatory attitude. In short, the relations between faith and reason and, in consequence, between philosophical knowledge and religious wisdom, were necessary problems for Islamism and Judaism, just as they were for Christianity.

Arabian philosophy was dominated by two great figures, Avicenna and Averroes.

Ibn Sina (in Latin *Avicenna*), who died in 1037, combined Aristotelianism and neo-Platonism in his system, using the metaphysics of Plotinus as a setting for Aristotle's logic and physics. This mingling of two philosophies so very opposed to each other in their inspiration and method was one of the characteristics common to almost all the Arab and Jewish thinkers. It can no doubt be explained by the fact that they had to make use of neo-Platonism to fill in the gaps left by Aristotle in his metaphysics and theology. However, the process was helped to no small degree by a simple fact of literary history: two neo-Platonic writings, one from Plotinus and the other from Proclus, had slipped into the catalogue of the works of Aristotle. The former work was known as the *Theology of Aristotle*, while the other was the famous *Liber de*

*Causis*, which the Latin world was to make so much of. This caused the Arab and Jewish philosophers to attribute the most original themes of neo-Platonism to Aristotle.

Avicenna bequeathed to the Christian West an encyclopaedic work, which is a vast paraphrase of the writings of Aristotle, completed by a neo-Platonic interpretation of creative causality. God, the eternal principle, the one, sovereign and perfect, is the eternal cause of a single effect, the first Intelligence. From the first Intelligence proceeds the second Intelligence, together with the first celestial sphere, which is an animated body moved by the first Intelligence. In its turn, the second Intelligence produces the third Intelligence, at the same time producing the second sphere and acting as its principle of movement. The emanation proceeds in this way as far as the last Intelligence, which is the *active* Intellect of mankind, the immediate principle of human souls and of the whole sublunary world. In this world, which is the kingdom of contingent beings, the knowledge and providence of the active Intellect is all that matters, for the divine knowledge is concerned only with universal principles. Avicenna's creationist metaphysics enables him to give an answer to the problem of human souls similar in many ways to that later proposed by St. Thomas, but his idea of the union of soul and body is Platonic and he therefore avoids one of the thorniest problems in Aristotelian psychology, that of the substantial union of the spiritual soul and matter.

Ibn Roschd (Averroes), who died in 1198, put the final touch to the triumph of Aristotle in Arabian philosophy. His admiration for Aristotle did not fall far short of actual worship. In addition to his own original writings, he left to posterity three series of commentaries on the books of Aristotle, which were to have a profound effect on the Latin world in its interpretation of the Philosopher. The commentaries were also to earn him the title of *Commentator*.

In his metaphysics, Averroes sees God as the one and only creative cause of all that is distinct from him. Not only does he recognize the creative causality of God, but he also attributes this doctrine to Aristotle, dismissing the opinion that God is only a motory cause as "the very depth of absurdity". Averroes' teaching is therefore in no way pantheistic; all creatures are composed of act and potency and are therefore distinct from God who alone is pure Act. The supreme Being eternally and immediately produces all Intelligences and all material species. The created universe, like its cause, is eternal. The pure Act does not know the world of generation and corruption and therefore does not govern it by its providence. Cosmic evolution results from the action of physical agents on matter, which possesses all forms in potency.

In psychology, Averroes interprets Aristotle's doctrine according to his famous theory of monopsychism. Man is a superior animal, who is born and dies like the animals, but whose brain is able to serve as an instrument of the "active" Intellect and of the "material" Intellect of the human species. The intellectual activity, which is exercised in different ways in human individuals, has for its principles two separate or immaterial substances, two subsistent forms which are eternal and incorruptible. They are the "active" Intellect, which is the last of the celestial Intelligences and which moves the lunar sphere, and the "material" or receptive Intellect, which receives into itself the intelligible forms abstracted by the active Intellect. Being situated on the boundaries of the spiritual world, these two Intellects have an activity of abstraction in which they unite themselves with individual human beings. For it is the "phantasms" or brain images of these same individuals which the active Intellect takes as its object in the process of abstraction, and they also determine specifically the receptive Intellect's operation. It is precisely inasmuch as the receptive Intellect is active in us, that we are conscious of thinking. Spirituality and immortality do not belong to individuals, but only to the Intellect of the human species. It is easy enough to get some idea of the moral and social consequences of such a doctrine which, at the human level, is materialism of the most radical kind.

On the whole, the work of Averroes marks a return to the authentic Aristotelianism and is also a reaction against neo-Platonic philosophy. All the same, the Aristotelianism of the Commentator, by comparison with that of Aristotle himself, has some explanations and additions of considerable importance, especially in metaphysics (creative causality) and psychology (monopsychism).

The Arab philosophy has a remarkable parallel in the philosophy developed by the Jews of the Arab world. Here also a conflict arises between the philosophers and the more conservatively minded guardians of the Law and the rabbinical traditions. Here also, two figures tower above all others in the influence which they had over the thirteenth century Christian world —Avicebron and Maimonides.

Solomon Ibn Gebirol, known to the Latin world as Avicebron, was a contemporary of St. Anselm: he lived at Saragossa in the eleventh century († 1070), and is the author of a philosophical treatise entitled *The Fount of Life* (*Fons Vitae*). His doctrine is quite clearly neo-Platonic, the most characteristic thesis being that of universal hylomorphism—all creatures, spiritual as well as corporeal, are composed of matter and form. In accordance with the system of Plotinus, he grafts on to this fundamental idea both a conception of the hierarchy of forms, corresponding to the hierarchy of material principles, and also the explanation of universal change by a process of emanation which is intellectual in character, resulting as it does from the illumination or impression made on matter by the superior Intelligences.

Moses Maimonides is the great Jewish thinker of the twelfth century. A contemporary of Averroes, he was born like him at Cordova and died in Egypt in 1205. His *Guide for the Doubting* is a *summa* of religious speculations. Like Averroes, he returns to the teaching of Aristotle, but the brand of Aristotelianism which he professes has a touch of neo-Platonism about it, often inspired by Avicenna. The problem of the relations between philosophy and religion is of vital interest to him and he conceives of philosophy as being above all an instrument for theological speculation, its object being to throw light on the obscure pages of Holy Writ. Maimonides also recognizes the weaknesses in Aristotelian doctrine and opposes the biblical notion of Providence to the naturalism of the Philosopher. In general, the position he holds is often quite like that of St. Thomas.

\* \* \*

Having made this rapid examination of the intellectual attainments of the Greeks and Arabs, we are
now in a position to determine how much work of
assimilation would be required of the Christian world
in the thirteenth century. It is in this period, thanks
to a vast influx of foreign literary material, that the
Latin West benefited for the first time from almost
all the contents of the intellectual storehouse of two
civilizations, Greek and Arab. If we are to understand
the bewilderment caused by the new philosophical
literature, it is essential that we should first call to
mind the intellectual atmosphere which obtained in
the Christian world towards the end of the twelfth
century.

# CHAPTER II

# THE STATE OF PHILOSOPHY IN THE TWELFTH CENTURY

European civilization, says Mandonnet, from the first attempts of the Barbarians to form social units until the end of the Renaissance, was built up chiefly by the restoration and absorption of the Greco-Roman civilization. For ten centuries, Europe was the disciple of antiquity, borrowing and slowly adapting to its own needs almost the whole of this ancient culture. This work of assimilation was accomplished in three successive stages. First, the institutions of antiquity were taken into the system, the first Renaissance culminating in the restoration of the Empire (by Charlemagne) and of Roman Law. In the twelfth and thirteenth centuries came the assimilation of Greek science and philosophy, and the fourteenth, fifteenth and sixteenth centuries finished the process by borrowing their literary and artistic forms from the ancient world.

Until the twelfth century, the young medieval society had exploited the cultural heritage of Rome especially. With the Church as their guide and taught by the Fathers and first Doctors of the Faith, they had adopted the language of the Romans and had found, in classical Latin literature, models for rhetoric, poetry and history, some philosophical ideas and some moral, social and pedagogic notions. These had first borne fruit at the time of the Carolingian Renaissance and were to set a humanist stamp on the Renaissance of the twelfth century. However, the influence of the Greek world during this long period had not been negligible. Such men as Chalcidius, Marius Victorinus, Macrobius and St. Augustine had transmitted to the Middle Ages an important legacy of Platonic and neo-Platonic ideas; while Boethius had had the distinction of introducing Aristotle to the West and was responsible for the authority enjoyed by Aristotle's Logic in the intellectual training of the men of the High Middle Ages.

The twelfth century was able to make use of all these intellectual riches and to increase them by the addition of new treasures, thanks to the increasing frequency of contact with the Byzantine and Moslem worlds. After the slow preparations of the preceding ages, civilization sprang into activity in the twelfth century and this brillant renascence has been called by De Wulf "the springtime of feudal civilization". And further on: "the freshness of youth now bursts forth in all forms of human activity". It was a social and economic renascence, with its chivalry and the beginnings of the emancipation of a town-bourgeoisie; a religious renascence with the crusades, the monastic reform of Cîteaux and the creation of new religious orders; finally it was a renascence in letters, in the arts and in the sciences. However, twelfth-century medieval thought had not yet reached the maturity of creation and synthesis, for it was still at the stage of *assimilation*. It was only with difficulty that the twelfth century managed to master the sources of its intellectual life; it was living on the

heritage of the ancients, rather than on new achieve-
ments; there was renewed awareness of the eternal
problems concerning man, the world and God, but
the attempted solutions which it rediscovered among
the treasures of antiquity, or which it itself but
dimly caught sight of, were lacking in breadth
and solidity. Whether we are dealing with the
group of Chartres or of Saint-Victor, with an Abelard or with a John of Salisbury, we always come up
against this same fault in systematization, although
we can, it is true, speak of partial syntheses, and lay
some stress on the remarkable efforts made by these
thinkers in their attempt to attain a comprehensive interpretation of reality. "The Scholastics of the
first period", wrote De Wulf, "were unable to reconcile the contradictory doctrines to which they
were attracted, powerless to go beyond them or correct them. A lack of cohesion affects, to a greater
or less extent, all philosophical productions from the
ninth century to the end of the twelfth, and even
the better among them are not exempt from this
fault. John of Salisbury could have applied to all the
men of his time what he wrote in the *Metalogicus* (II,
17) about the efforts of the school of Chartres to reconcile Plato and Aristotle: 'They laboured in vain
to reconcile dead men, who all their life had been at
variance' ".

It was then a period of assimilation, of receptivity
and consequently of eclecticism. This is the all-im-
portant factor which dominates the history of the
High Middle Ages to the end of the twelfth century
and it is this which explains the relative poverty of
these long centuries in philosophical production properly so-called.

Another very important fact contributes something to the explanation of the slowness of philosophical progress before the thirteenth century, namely, the *primacy of theology* in the Christian conception of knowledge. This fact, which is of capital importance in the history of our culture, has not gone unperceived. All attempts to interpret medieval thought concentrate on this point, for it constitutes one of the principal data for the problem of Christian humanism in its intellectual aspect, the problem, that is, of the relations between faith and reason. But the encounter between Christian doctrine and philosophical reasoning has given rise to interpretations and above all to judgments so divergent, that we are obliged to indicate here the angle from which we shall view the problem, defining our position exactly, so as to avoid all equivocation and quibbling over terminology.

Without any doubt, these complex questions can be made much clearer if we learn to appreciate the fact that the term "philosophy" has, even in current language, two meanings which we must distinguish with care, while not forgetting that they have a common root. Taken in its strictest sense, the term "philosophy" designates a definite *scientific discipline* which, starting from principles recognized as evident and with the aid of critically defined methods, has as its goal the construction of a systematic interpretation of the universal order. In a much wider sense, we can give the name "philosophy" to any general conception of the world and of human life, any group of ideas concerned with the mysteries of existence, and even any concrete attitude of man towards them; in short, any *synthetic view of the universe*.

While "scientific" philosophy is found, like the other elements of the scientific life, only in the more advanced cultural circles, it exists in its wider signif-ication at every level of civilization and therefore appears in very different forms. It is found mixed up with all the other cultural elements (religion, art, literature, customs etc.) and is normally concerned with man seen concretely under every aspect, not only in his intellectual life, but also in his affective life and social attitudes. In circles where "scientific" philos-ophy is well established, the philosophical movement properly so-called merges completely with philoso-phy in the wide sense of the word. It is this philoso-phy which precedes and paves the way for "scientific" philosophy, in that it represents the pre-philosophical attitude of the man without culture. It accompanies the true philosophy, acting as its support and as a psychological stimulant in the mind of the profes-sional philosopher. It completes and crowns technical philosophy, both as a comprehensive sum of know-ledge and as a practical outlook on life in the mind of the cultured man. In Greek antiquity, for instance, the literary work of Aristotle is an outstanding exam-ple of "scientific" philosophy, but clearly this work has to be inserted in a much wider philosophical con-text, when one considers it in relation to the personal thought of Aristotle or of his contemporaries. Aris-totle's philosophy is one of the scientific monuments in which the world outlook of the ancient Greeks is formulated.

Having made this distinction, we can now turn to the Christian world. For anybody who accepts the message of the gospel, the true view of the universe can henceforward be nothing but a Christian view.

For the Christian, philosophy, understood as a *Welt-anschauung*, is necessarily subject to the authority of faith or, to be more exact, to the authority of divine Revelation, which is the object of faith. The Christian's comprehensive sum of knowledge and practical attitude to problems set by existence are dominated by the outlook of faith; this Christian wisdom positively excludes any purely human wisdom which might claim to be the supreme standard for thought and action. On the other hand, a fully developed Christian civilization ought among other things to include an intellectual life, at the heart of which all forms of knowledge could themselves develop—must develop, even—according to their own laws. For the human elements of a civilization are neither suppressed nor distorted by Christianity. On the contrary, they all contribute to the realization of the ideal of Christian humanism and, consequently, "scientific" philosophy finds its place beside theology and the positive sciences in a complete organization of the intellectual life in a Christian atmosphere. Taken all together, these sciences, when duly co-ordinated and graded according to their respective objects and methods, tend towards the unification of the whole of human knowledge in a supreme synthesis. In short, this would be a higher theology, or a specifically Christian *Welt-anschauung*, or even the supreme synthesis of philosophy and theology, the comprehensive Christian sum of knowledge.

Now that these notions have been clarified, the interpretation of the historical development of human thought becomes much easier.

It is evident that the origins of Christianity had nothing to do with the intellectual movement of

Greece and have scarcely any relationship with the history of "scientific" philosophy. The teaching of Christ and of the apostles did not express any philosophical system; it announced rather the "good news" of the salvation of all men, learned and ignorant, and invited them to a new mode of life, inspired by the teachings of Revelation. On the other hand, the coming of Christianity marked a radical change in the philosophical ideas which went to make up the world outlook of the pagans and even of the Jews; it implied the substitution of the Christian *Weltanschauung* for those of paganism and of Judaism. As a reaction against the earthly messianism of the Jews and the materialism prevailing in pagan society, primitive Christianity so expressed the Christian ideal as to lay great stress on the eternal destiny of souls. It preached the need to seek for the one thing necessary and to hold transitory things in contempt; it opposed the humble acceptance of divine truth by faith, to the arrogant wisdom of the world. In short, the message of Christ announced a humanism of the most sublime kind, in inviting men to a divine destiny and conferring on the human person a supernatural value. It was a glaring contradiction, at first sight, to humanism as it is understood nowadays, for it seemed to oblige men to scorn all *provisional* or *transitory* human values, namely riches, pleasures, honours, wisdom.

However, the Christian life begins here below and consequently this earthly habitation of ours must be organized in such a way as to ensure that men will enjoy all the conditions of life which are necessary if they are to be able to work out to the full their personal destiny. Owing to the force of circumstances, the problem of humanism presented itself to the

Christian communities from the very beginning. The question became more and more varied as the Church grew, and history shows that once the essential was assured, the Church did all it could to foster the development of civilization, becoming the, great educator of the new world which emerged after the destruction of the Roman Empire and the barbarian invasions.

At the level of the intellectual life, there appears the same contrast between the primitive Christian preaching and the later practice of the Church. The first generations of Christians felt that their main obligation was to react against the intellectual pride and the wisdom of the philosophers, so as to establish firmly a supernatural outlook, illumined by faith in the word of God. While making use of the results of Greek knowledge to a varied extent, the Christians of the first centuries readily set their Christian wisdom in opposition to that of the pagans. When Christianity found itself for the first time in the presence of neo-Platonism, which was not only a powerful philosophical synthesis, but also a moral and mystical way of life, the first contacts were by no means peaceful. Porphyry in particular proved himself a decided opponent of the Christians. Before long, however, though it was bitterly opposed to the message of salvation, this neo-Platonism became the very core of Augustinian philosophy, and Christian thought took a prodigious leap forward with the work of that great intellectual, St Augustine.

All the same, the Bishop of Hippo did not repudiate the primacy of faith over reason, nor that of Christian wisdom over human wisdom. For him the "true philosophy", the true "love of wisdom", coincides with the love of God, and real wisdom is that which is illuminated by the lamp of faith, a lamp kept lit by the Incarnate Word. For human reason will surely go astray if left to its own devices. On the other hand, the work of St. Augustine is not that of a professor or of one who was a professional in scientific work and it does not in any way indicate that he was at all concerned with technique or methodology. It is the work of a convert, a pastor of a flock, an apologist. As a doctor of the faith, Augustine worked tirelessly to reveal, elaborate and defend the sum of Christian wisdom, which he contrasted with the false wisdom of pagan philosophers. Far from underlining the relative autonomy of the various sciences, he took pleasure in emphasizing the fatal deficiencies of reason when left to its natural powers. In short, in the work of St. Augustine, Christian thought had not yet reached the stage of scientific organization; its unity was less a unity of order than that of a body of knowledge as yet undifferentiated. The synthesis achieved by the Bishop of Hippo was wholly theological.

St. Augustine was the leading authority in the intellectual formation of the Latin Church, in which his influence was preponderant until the thirteenth century and even beyond. Thus, the Augustinian conception of a unique wisdom issuing from faith was commonly accepted during the whole of the High Middle Ages. As the organization of education developed and the process of differentiation between the various sciences began to evolve, so this Augustinian conception of knowledge tended to group all the profane sciences around theology, the sacred science. The definite triumph of Christianity over paganism in Western Europe and the clergy's monopoly in education each played a part in ensuring that theology should hold the undisputed supremacy in the intellectual life of this period. Knowledge developed only in the line of faith, according to the Augustinian formula: *crede ut intelligas*. Faith comes first, because it is a participation in God's own knowledge, and before this divine knowledge mere human knowledge must bow. The formula of St. Anselm, *fides quaerens intellectum*, is a repetition of that of St. Augustine, and this formula, which very happily expresses the movement of theological thought, at the same time sums up the entire intellectual life of the first twelve centuries of our era. We need only consider the doctrines contained in germ in the New Testament, or the apologetic work of the first Christian controversialists in the second and third centuries, or the literature of theological polemics aroused by the great fourth and fifth century heresies, or the imposing doctrinal synthesis built up by St. Augustine, or the "scholastic" theology (that is, the theology of the schools), which gradually developed after the Carolingian Renaissance. In all of these, we meet with a knowledge which is specifically Christian, illumined by faith and organized with Revelation as its centre.

We must admit that this preponderance of theology in academic circles retarded the development of philosophy. For in offering the Christian outlook to the minds of men, and in proposing an explanation of the universe which gave a meaning to the life of the person and to the history of mankind, the Church satisfied man's natural curiosity concerning the problems of his origin and destiny, and by that same token suppressed one of the fundamental stimuli to-

wards philosophical research. Moreover, in directing
men of study towards the sacred science, she inevitably turned them aside from work which was properly
philosophical.

It might be objected that, although interest in speculative problems may have lessened, as far as the anguish
of the philosopher was concerned, because of the light
thrown by Revelation on the solution of the problem
of the universe, yet it may well have found a new
and no less efficient stimulus in the Christian mystery
itself. The classical formulas of Augustinianism, *credo
ut intelligam* and *fides quaerens intellectum*, might
once more be invoked in support of the theory that
the intelligence of the Christian, just as much as that
of the pagan, preserved a reverence and a love of
truth. These observations appear to be just, but they
do not invalidate what we have said concerning philosophical effort in the strict sense. From the point of
view of methods and needs which are specific to rational research, it is an undeniable fact that the predominance of a preoccupation with theology slowed
the advance of philosophy during the first twelve centuries of the Christian era.

Still, it would be wrong to conclude that the High
Middle Ages had no knowledge or appreciation of
profane learning. After St. Augustine and Boethius,
all the Scholastics, from the ninth to the twelfth
century, exploited the literary heritage of antiquity
and made a place for the profane sciences in Christian
knowledge in its broadest sense. In the twelfth century, theology was undoubtedly enthroned at the
summit of *philosophia*, that is, of wisdom as a whole,
but it was surrounded by the seven liberal arts, which

were the maids-in-waiting of the queen of sciences [1].
If they had to serve her, it was because they were indispensable to the sacred science as auxiliaries in her
perfect development; hence the theologians, seeing
that it was in the interest of their science, were
prompted to bring the profane sciences to the fore,
so as to be sure of having better tools at hand for
the accomplishment of their task. We meet with
ideas such as these in a man like Abelard, who cultivated his beloved logic with a view to putting it at the
disposal of theology. Others followed him in this
path and, like him, laid stress on the speculative character of the sacred science, while more conservative
circles were doing their best to shield it from philosophical influence.

What then is to be reckoned in the twelfth century
philosophical balance-sheet ? The upsurge of interest
in dialectics, of which Abelard is the very incarnation, secured the triumph of Aristotle in logic and
introduced his theory of knowledge into the schools,
thus giving a foretaste of his overall triumph in the
following century. Abelard fixed once and for all the
characteristics of the scholastic method, thereby settling decisively the direction which speculative theology was to take. Other philosophical tendencies also
began to take shape in the schools during the twelfth
century. At Chartres, the dependence of the Middle
Ages on antiquity in matters of culture was keenly
felt, and this stimulated classical studies and provoked
not only the production of works on dialectics, but

[1] Before the thirteenth century, the whole of learning, including both the human sciences and the divine or theological
science, was called *philosophia*. This term denoted the whole of
Christian wisdom, as with St. Augustine.

also a return to the Platonic themes of the *Timaeus*. Metaphysics began to head for pantheism and there was a revival of interest in mathematics and the natural sciences. At Saint-Victor, which was a centre of intense theological and mystical studies, various philosophical questions came into the limelight, among them being the classification of the sciences, psychological problems and questions of natural theology. Remarkable men like John of Salisbury soon brought fame to their schools. The school of Gilbert of la Porrée (Simon of Tournai, Alan of Lille) imparted a new development to certain branches of philosophy, incorporating the views of Aristotle in its theological expositions. The twelfth century was thus a century of renewal, witnessing as it did a great intellectual activity and a lively scientific curiosity.

In the light of present day knowledge, therefore, there can no longer be any question of reducing the philosophy of the twelfth century to a few ideas on logic, or to the controversy over universals, as was the tendency in the past. Not only was philosophy studied during this period outside the schools of the liberal arts (where it was reduced, in principle, to dialectics), but it is an established fact that, from the twelfth century, the classical programme of the seven arts was expanded in certain quarters. For example, the teaching of philosophy at Chartres plainly went beyond the bounds of dialectics and a large part was left, broadly speaking, to the initiative and preferences of the masters.

Yet, despite their undeniable merits, the thinkers of the twelfth century still displayed the two following shortcomings and both were of considerable importance for the future. In the first place, the philosoph-

ical literature of this period bears witness to the preponderant, or (in some places) exclusive place taken
by *dialectics* in the teaching of philosophy. Secondly,
even when this teaching passed beyond the limits of
dialectics, in order to include problems of natural philosophy, metaphysics and ethics, it remained *fragmentary* and, as it were, incidental; it remained eclectic
and never rose to the level of knowledge with a universal object, for it knew nothing of the all-embracing
pretensions of a philosophical system.

We can put this summary of the intellectual life of
the twelfth century into a more concrete form, if we
take a look at Paris, as it was during the quarter of
a century preceding the foundation of the university
(by the charter of Philip Augustus in the year 1200).
Here we find a great number of schools, those of the
liberal arts and of theology being the most highly
esteemed, and it is only with these that we shall here
concern ourselves. The grouping of the arts schools
is soon to give rise to the *Facultas artium*, while the
schools of theology are to form the *Facultas theologiae*. What do we find happening in this twofold
centre of learning and how must we picture the main
trends of the teaching which is given there ?

In the arts schools of Paris, where, more than in
any other place, the memory of Abelard seems to have
inspired a continued devotion to dialectics, the teaching of philosophy, if we are to judge by the literature
it produced, is confined to the explanation of the
treatises of the *Organon* and of the other works on
logic which have become classical. This theoretical and
practical initiation into Aristotelian logic is the crown-
ing point of a syllabus which embraces the exact

sciences and the literary subjects, that is, the *quadrivium* and the *trivium*. Thus, these schools of the liberal arts are centres of profane studies, whose programme is quite distinct from that of the schools of theology. A school of liberal arts is more or less a preparatory school, where one acquires the general culture needed before taking up studies of a more specialized nature. The philosophical training there received aims at exercising the intelligence rather than furnishing it with information, and it includes nothing resembling a philosophical view of the universe. The teaching of the arts is so far from being an end in itself that the masters do not normally make a definite career of it, but use it as a stage where they can pass some years of their youth, before going on to fill higher offices.

Now what do we find in the schools of theology ? Here, we discover that the students are young clerics, who have worked their way through the cycle of the liberal arts and who now aspire to higher intellectual conquests. The masters also have fought their first campaigns in the arts and, as we have seen, the booty and philosophical "impedimenta" which they have carried away from the fray are not very cumbersome. Moreover, their teaching of theology is centred, not on philosophical speculation, but much more, as is only fitting, on the inspired text of the Bible and on the writings of the Fathers. We shall not describe in detail the state of theological studies at the end of the twelfth century, a period so prolific in this field. Nor is it our intention to recall how there were added to the literal commentary on the Holy Scriptures, first glosses, then the compilations of "sentences", then the "*summae*" of a yet more complex structure. Moreover, we shall not mention how the dialectical method gradually compelled a recognition equal to that given to the *auctoritates*. In short, we do not mean to describe the laborious ways by which the organization and systematization of the sacred science, as witnessed by the twelfth century, were accomplished. But what we must do is to bring to the foreground some of the characteristics affecting theological knowledge around 1200, such as are displayed in the theological literature of this period.

On the whole, this literature belongs to what today we should call positive theology, rather than to speculative theology. At the end of the twelfth century, theologians were more concerned with determining the data of Revelation and exploiting the evidence of the patristic tradition, than with philosophical discussion on the meaning of religious truths. The role of dialectics in this positive teaching is not so much doctrinal as formal or methodological. As to the philosophical treatment of the revealed data by the speculative method, it remained fragmentary and played only a subordinate part during the whole of the twelfth century. Doubtless, this new use of dialectics in theology had found determined and at times dangerous supporters among famous masters such as Roscelin, Abelard, William of Conches and Gilbert of la Porrée [1]. But a strong reaction against the inroads made by philosophy into sacred doctrine was not slow in asserting itself, particularly among the disciples of Peter Lombard and among the Victorines in Paris. Mgr. Grabmann gathered together a series of declar-

[1] Until the Lateran Council (1215), the school of Gilbert of la Porrée was a dangerous rival of the Augustinian school descending from Peter Lombard.

ations hostile to Aristotle dating from the twelfth century. He has shown that many theologians at the end of the twelfth and at the beginning of the thirteenth century displayed conservative tendencies. They applied themselves to the study of Holy Scripture and, without neglecting dogmatic theology, they took a lively interest in the practical problems of moral and sacramental theology. Often we find that their writings have an eye to the needs of the pastoral ministry, but the influence of the "new philosophy" is scarcely ever apparent.

In actual fact, speculative theology produced no real doctrinal synthesis before the thirteenth century. The second half of the twelfth century abounded in collections of sentences and theological "*summae*", but although these were compiled from materials organized to a more or less rational theological plan, they still did not conform to the requirements of rigorous systematization. Still harder to find is a philosophical synthesis placed at the service of Christian doctrine. In short, where theological speculation did appear, it was eclectic in its inspiration. St. Augustine was its principal source, but it did not scorn the use of other sources, especially Aristotle and Pseudo-Dionysius.

From the foregoing examination of facts some important consequences can be drawn.

The first is that *no definite philosophical trends existed at the end of the twelfth century*, either in the schools of liberal arts, or anywhere else. There did exist, especially in Paris, a vivid interest both in the *study of dialectics*, inspired principally by Aristotle's *Organon*, and in *theological studies*. The latter, in so far as they made use of the speculative method, depended on a variety of philosophical elements. But strictly speaking, neither Aristotelianism nor Augustinianism had yet become an organized *philosophical system* or a definite trend in doctrine. The assimilation of the systems of antiquity—Platonism, Aristotelianism, neo-Platonism in all its forms, including philosophical Augustinianism—is still found to be too incomplete for us to be able to speak so early of a true renascence of these systems and still less can there be any question of creations whose originality would reflect the genius proper to the thinkers of the Middle Ages. In this also, it is the thirteenth century which is to see the emancipation of the mind and which will produce the first really personal works of Scholasticism [1].

[1] Fr. Mandonnet seems to us to go too far when he writes: "The most important manifestations of the civilizations of Europe have nothing fundamentally original about them until the end of Humanism". Before the sixteenth century, he continues, "the original elements in the culture of the Middle Ages are still in the background, being hidden or supplanted by foreign elements. In the political and social sphere, originality shows itself in the communal movement and all that follows from it; in intellectual life, it consists in the awakening of the critical sense and the spirit of observation; and in aesthetics, it is represented by Gothic art and by the first attempts to use the national languages in literature". (*Siger de Brabant*, 2nd ed., vol.I, Louvain, 1911, p. 2). This minimises too much the part played in medieval culture by new factors such as the influence of Christianity and the contributions made by the barbaric peoples, not to mention the personal effort of the men who forged the Europe of the Middle Ages. On the social plane, we must mention the fact that feudalism and chivalry, the activity of the monks and the efforts to organize charity, all occurred before the communal movement. On the plane of the intellectual life, the necessary corrections to Fr. Mandonnet's thesis can be found in E. GILSON's *Spirit of Medieval Philosophy* (translated by A.H.C. DOWNES, Sheed and Ward, London, 1950).

We can now see in what sense we can speak of 'Augustinianism" with regard to the intellectual movement of the twelfth century. In the first place, twelfth century *philosophy,* understood as *a synthetic vision of the universe,* was essentially Christian and Augustinian. Besides, the Latin *theology* of the High Middle Ages was quite plainly Augustinian, for beyond all question St. Augustine was its chief inspiration; he was the author most quoted and most used in every department of the sacred science. Moreover, western theology remained Augustinian, not only until St. Thomas, but even in the Thomistic theology itself, and it is still Augustinian today to a large extent. However, if we look at the twelfth century from the point of view of *scientific philosophy,* it would be very inaccurate to speak of Augustinianism. Whether we consider the fragmentary nature of philosophical endeavour in the schools of liberal arts, or the first speculations of the theologians, or the philosophical sources used by the scholastics of this century, we cannot but appreciate the fact that an Augustinian philosophy did not exist in this period. The terminology, principles, argumentations and doctrines which make up the texture of twelfth century thought betray an eclectic inspiration. In reality, philosophy was not yet constituted as a distinct science and the philosophical elements which nourished intellectual life were much less homogeneous than they were in the thought of St. Augustine himself.

There is another corollary to the facts we have brought forward. In a milieu such as that of the Parisian schools of the end of the twelfth century, there could be no question of a *philosophical* rivalry or a *doctrinal* conflict between the schools of the liberal arts and the schools of theology; for both lacked any philosophical synthesis. The theologians had themselves been trained in dialectics in the schools of the liberal arts and could not look on them as something foreign, still less as rival or hostile institutions. The truth was that the arts schools like the theology schools had only one view of the universe, and that the Christian view. The most we can say is that a certain number of theologians protested, in the name of this common Christian wisdom, against an excessive craze for dialectics or for the other profane sciences. But the formation of real philosophical schools and definite trends in doctrine was left to the thirteenth century. This privilege was to be mainly Aristotle's.

# CHAPTER III

# THE PHILOSOPHICAL MOVEMENT IN THE THIRTEENTH CENTURY STATE OF THE QUESTION

In spite of the accumulation, during the past hundred years, of innumerable historical works, all trying to draw a faithful picture of medieval thought, this vast subject of study is still far from being exhausted. With regard to the study of the great century of scholasticism, we can get some idea of the results achieved and of the path which must still be trod, by reading the volume devoted to this brilliant period by M. De Wulf in the last edition of his *Histoire de la Philosophie Médiévale* [1]. In fact, if one compares this with the preceding edition, some twelve years previous (1924-25), it is surprising to see how many new masters have appeared, how many problems of criticism have found their solution and to what degree certain historical perspectives have had to be modified. But the prolific nature of medieval studies also helps to show up the enormous gaps in our knowledge of the thirteenth century. We shall therefore take a rapid glance through M. De Wulf's book, pointing out the work which still has to be done.

[1] M. DE WULF, *Histoire de la Philosophie Médiévale*, 6th edition, vol. 2, 1936: *Le Treizième Siècle*. (English translation, E. C. MESSENGER, *History of Medieval Philosophy*, vol. 2, London, 1938).

The intellectual life of the thirteenth century was dominated by one prime historical fact: the introduction into the West of an abundance of philosophical and scientific literature, Greek, Jewish and Arabian in origin, in successive waves from the mid-twelfth to the mid-thirteenth century. The history of this surge of translations, from Arabic to Latin and from Greek to Latin, still presents us with a vast field for research, even at this present day. Besides the certain conclusions already reached, there still remain to be solved a great number of questions about the origin, the date, the circumstances of composition, the literary dependence and the value of the translations.

The provision of critical editions of these medieval translations, which were the principal sources for the Latin philosophers of the Middle Ages, is one of the most urgent scientific undertakings incumbent on us at the present time. This need has been recognized and the ambitious plan of the *International Academic Union* to create a *Corpus Philosophorum Medii Aevi* is at this moment limited, as far as immediate realization of the project goes, to three undertakings, all of which have the Latin translations of the Middle Ages as their object.

The first of these is the *Aristoteles Latinus*, the critical edition of translations of Aristotle from Greek to Latin. The preliminary work is far advanced and some of the collaborators have already managed to establish critical editions of the texts entrusted to them. On the whole, however, we are still a long way from our goal. Up to date, only four volumes have appeared, the first in 1939, the second in 1951, the other two in 1953.

The *Mediaeval Academy of America* is concentrating on a second enterprise, the *Averroes Latinus*—the critical edition of Latin versions of Averroes and of Latin translations of Aristotle from Arabic. The first volume of the *Corpus Commentariorum Averrois in Aristotelem* appeared in 1949, the second in 1953.

Finally, the *Corpus Platonicum Medii Aevi*, which is being published by the *Academic Union* in collaboration with the British Academy, will consist of a *Plato Latinus* and a *Plato Arabus*; the work is entrusted to the Warburg Institute in London. Three volumes have appeared in the *Plato Latinus* (1940, 1950, 1953), and two in the *Plato Arabus* (1943, 1945).

The *Arts Faculty* of Paris and the other equivalent centres in Oxford, Naples, Sienna, etc., are of primary importance in the history of philosophy and in the history of thirteenth century Aristotelianism in particular. The history of these places of learning, which was practically non-existent thirty years ago, has since made considerable progress, due principally to the researches of Mgr. Grabmann. Unknown personalities have come to the fore, a wealth of literature has seen the light of day, and the direction which these masters took is becoming clearer. But these first rough outlines are only a modest beginning in comparison with the results which we may expect in the near future, as regards both the editing of texts and the history of literature and doctrine.

Similar reflections could be made on the subject of the different schools making up the *Faculties of Theology*, whether secular, Franciscan, Dominican, Cistercian or of any other religious order. Although the theological literature of the Middle Ages has, up to the present, been examined much more than the

strictly philosophical literature, there is still an enormous amount of work to be done, and it concerns not
only second and third rate men, but also the greatest
masters of the century. It will be sufficient to recall
that our editions of Albert the Great and of Duns
Scotus are still very defective [1], while almost all the
writings of Thomas of York, Gerard of Abbeville,
Roland of Cremona, Hugh of St. Cher, Richard Fishacre, Robert Kilwardby, Ulrich of Strasbourg, James
of Viterbo and many others have not yet been edited.
Problems of literary history are still to be met with at
every step in the case of the theologians, even the
greatest of them.

We must therefore make our approach through the
still badly defined roads of a city which is still being
built. We shall have to clear a passage for ourselves,
through the heaps of materials which stand on all
sides, and in order to find a site for our own building
among this ever-changing muddle, we shall have to
discover the city's principal avenues and cross-roads
for ourselves. However, the work of our predecessors
will be a great help towards the realization of our
task, and that is our reason for giving the following
general description of the results of their researches.

The innumerable monographs which have appeared
on the thirteenth century have revealed, bit by bit,
what a complex and living reality it was. They bring
us nearer to the objective which historians of the past

[1] The first volume of the critical edition of Albert the Great's
works appeared in 1951 (Cologne), the second volume in 1952.
The critical edition of the works of Duns Scotus comprises at
present three volumes: vol. I and II appeared in 1950, vol. III
in 1954 (Rome).

hundred years have had before them, since the beginning of medieval research. Their aim has always been to build up a picture of the true intellectual character of this period and then to discover its deeper historical significance, by unravelling the skein of entangled influences and by determining the main doctrinal trends, which by their life and action largely explain the evolution of ideas in the golden age of scholasticism. To mark out the main stages in this historical reconstruction of the thirteenth century, we shall draw attention to a series of works which have a historical synthesis as their main concern.

The supremacy of Aristotle in the schools of philosophy and even in the schools of theology during the Middle Ages is not a recent discovery. The humanists and reformers gave this as one of their reasons for objecting to the scholastics, and it was against their accusation of undue servility to Aristotle that Talamo in 1873 undertook to defend the masters of the Middle Ages. His work, which is in the form of an *apologia* and is plainly below the present-day standards of scholarship, contains in outline some interesting ideas on the rebirth of Aristotelianism in a Christian atmosphere. The work was followed two years later by Schneid's German adaptation of it.

The era of critical research on the question of Aristotle's influence opened, in 1889, with the articles written by Ehrle (who later became a cardinal) on the conflict between *Augustinianism* and *Aristotelianism* in the thirteenth century. In these erudite investigations, Ehrle brings to light, for the first time, some aspects of the doctrinal battle which took place at Paris and Oxford in the second half of the thirteenth century. In this way, he draws attention to the two most powerful doctrinal currents which run through the whole of the Middle Ages and which are nourished at two of the most important sources of scholastic thought—Aristotle and St. Augustine.

Ten years later, in 1899, the work of Fr. Mandonnet marked a new stage in the unfolding of the character of the thirteenth century. Besides the *Platonic-Augustinian current* and *Christian Aristotelianism* (by which he meant the school of St. Albert and St. Thomas), Fr. Mandonnet distinguished a third school, that of *Averroistic Aristotelianism* or Latin Averroism. Renan had already revealed the fact that this school existed in the Middle Ages, but with regard to the thirteenth century his attempts at a reconstruction had remained very imperfect and rudimentary. As for the current "Augustinian Platonism", Fr. Mandonnet sees the thirteenth century Augustinians as heirs to the thought of St. Augustine and, beyond him, to that "philosophico-religious syncretism" which characterized Platonism and neo-Platonism. He draws attention to what he thinks is a distinctive trait in this tradition, namely the absence of any formal distinction between the field of philosophy and that of theology. He also discovers a marked preference for Plato, to the detriment of Aristotle.

Writing two years later, M. De Wulf argues that the term *Augustinianism* is not a very apt title for those doctrines which were characteristic of scholasticism in the first half of the thirteenth century. Instead he proposes "a more indefinite but more comprehensive title, such as the *Early Scholasticism* of the thirteenth century, or the *Pre-Thomistic School*".

Alongside these researches, various historians were engaged on the task of determining the influence of

*Platonism* and of *neo-Platonism* on the Middle Ages. Among others, we must recall the original and certainly exaggerated thesis of Picavet, according to which the real master of Christian scholastics was not Aristotle but Plotinus. It is to Picavet's credit that he drew attention to an essential aspect of medieval thought, for more recent research has revealed the important role played by neo-Platonism in the philosophical conceptions of the thirteenth century. Plotinus and Proclus exercised their influence in any number of ways upon both the Arab and the Latin worlds. In 1916 and 1917, Baeumker crowned a series of earlier monographs with two brilliant synthetical studies on medieval Platonism.

In 1915, there appeared a contribution of Dr. Schneider's to the history of Aristotelianism and Arabianism. The author upsets the hitherto accepted plan of things by his corrections and subtle distinctions. According to that plan the philosophical renascence dates from the thirteenth century and is due almost entirely to the new literature introduced towards the beginning of the period. He shows how the cultural renascence of the Middle Ages can be traced back to the twelfth century, even in the case of philosophy, for in the thirteenth century it merely underwent an intensification, thanks to the new translations. Moreover, the thirteenth century did not see the exclusive triumph of Aristotelianism over the more Platonic Augustinianism of the previous epoch. Augustinianism continued to hold its own in the thirteenth century in the face of Aristotelianism, which had in any case been important in the twelfth century, even outside the field of logic. The influence of Aristotelianism was due partly to direct acquaintance with Aristotle's

works, partly to Jewish, Arab and Latin intermediaries (especially Boethius).

M. De Wulf used to insist on the convergence of
the philosophical systems of the Middle Ages and he
thought it possible to pick out what he called for a
long time the *scholastic synthesis*, common to most of
the masters, at least in the thirteenth century. The
works of M. Gilson tend rather to lay the stress on
the variety of medieval trends in doctrine. Thus M.
Gilson strongly emphasizes the opposition between
Aristotelianism and Augustinianism, and many historians, such as Fr. Chenu in France, M. Hessen in Germany and M. Sassen in Holland, show a similar tendency. M. Gilson has also attempted to analyse the con-
stituent factors of thirteenth century Augustinianism.
For instance, he has brought into prominence the originality of *Franciscan Augustinianism*, a system of
which St. Bonaventure is the most typical representative. Besides this, he thinks he has distinguished the
existence of a doctrinal trend, parallel to that of *Aristotelian Augustinianism*, which he calls *Avicennian
Augustinianism*. The appositeness of this new classification was questioned by M. De Wulf. According to
him, M. Gilson had bestowed an exaggerated importance on the theory of knowledge, when he made the
doctrine of divine illumination the line of cleavage
between thirteenth century Aristotelianism and Augustinianism. M. De Wulf thought the division was
chiefly to be found in metaphysics, which means that
we should speak rather of *Avicebronian Augustinianism*, for Avicebron played a major part in the formation of pre-Thomistic metaphysics [1].

[1] M. Gilson and M.De Wulf actually use the phrases: "augus-
tinisme    aristotélisant . . . avicennisant . . . avicebronisant".    Thus

In 1931, there appeared two noteworthy studies on Averroism. As usual, that of Mgr. Grabmann made use of the treasures of inedited material; on the contrary Fr. Gorce's article was a synthetic study, in which the author's views were perhaps supported by too little factual evidence. Two years later, Fr. Gorce widened his perspectives and painted a veritable tableau-vivant which he himself described as a "bold experiment" and an "altogether provisional synthesis". In the work he develops a great many historical sketches; his original, sometimes quite unexpected, suggestions and his ingenious, though at times peculiar, comparisons constantly stimulate the curiosity of the reader. But in the places where the author has not followed his own inspiration, he shows too servile a dependence on earlier works, notably on that of Renan, to whom he gives far too much credit.

The works of M. Gilson and Fr. Gorce had emphasized the part played by the Arabs, particularly by Avicenna, in the formation of Latin thought. In 1934, Fr. de Vaux went a step further by trying to demonstrate, from the requisite texts, the existence of a specifically Avicennian doctrinal trend. His aim was to establish the fact that in the early thirteenth century we come across traces of a "Latin Avicennianism" analogous to the heterodox movement which developed later and which Renan called "Latin Averroism". Philosophers, he maintained, took over the whole of Avicenna's doctrine, even where it was incompatible with Christian thought.

our translation is not quite accurate, but it is preferable to the paraphrases which would be necessary to render them accurately: "with Aristotelian tendencies", for example, or "somewhat Aristotelian", etc. (Translator's note).

To finish off our brief sketch, we must mention the recent works of Mgr. Grabmann on *medieval Aristotelianism*. Besides an impressive series of monographs, to which we shall return later, this scholar, so tireless in research, published four studies of a more general nature on the Aristotelian renascence of the Middle Ages. The first of these deals with the relations between Church and State; the second is a polished-up exposition of the theme earlier dealt with by Talamo; the third is of a more technical character and describes the main works of reference and the literary and pedagogic procedure customarily adopted by those teaching Aristotle; the fourth and last study treats of the Church's reaction to the influence of Aristotelianism.

The problems of historical synthesis, in the matter of the doctrinal trends of the thirteenth century, are in their turn to be connected with still wider problems, namely those concerning the relations between Christian faith and reason and, in the last analysis, between Christianity and Humanism, in medieval times. These problems are so vast and so complex that we cannot consider making an extended examination of them here. Nevertheless we cannot avoid recalling, at least in their general outlines, the main positions taken by the historians of medieval thought with regard to these problems.

By "Humanism", we here mean any ideology, any system of doctrine, which proposes an ideal for human life, or aims at defining man's full perfection; or any programme for life and action and any social movement which strives to promote the development of mankind in every sphere. When, in relation to Humanism seen in this sense, we consider the historical fact of the rise and development of Christianity, we are at once confronted with some very important questions. If Christianity is a religious and moral doctrine, a programme for life and an organized social movement, is it by that same token a concrete form of Humanism ? Or is it, on the contrary, a deviation from the human ideal, a forgery or a diseased and unnatural form of the ideal ? Or is it, as it claims to be, a "superhumanism", a call to a superhuman life, an invitation to man to be divinized, a supernatural conception of human life ? The Christian answers to these questions are obviously for the most part diametrically opposed to those furnished by non-Christians, because all the answers presuppose a judgment on the origin and transcendence of Christianity. There can be little hope therefore of ever finding answers to these problems which all will accept.

At first sight, it might be thought that the problem of the relations between Humanism and Christianity could be dealt with from a purely historical point of view and that in this way a solution might be found to which all historians would subscribe. The historiography of works devoted to the origins of Christianity and to the Christian Middle Ages banishes any such illusion. Historians barely manage to agree on a certain number of undeniable historical facts, but when they start interpreting, evaluating, appreciating and passing judgment on those facts, the difference between the views of the Christians and those of the non-Christians appears as a yawning chasm.

The following are the main conclusions reached by the rationalist historians and critics, in the matter of the intellectual aspect of the problem of Christian Humanism, that is, the question of the relations between faith and reason. Christian doctrine, which is a collection of beliefs that are human in origin, had a considerable, but baneful, influence in the evolution of Western thought. With the coming of Christianity and especially of Catholicism, the advance of philosophy was brought to a full stop. Orthodoxy stifled all freedom of thought; faith, by offering a ready-made solution to the fundamental problems of philosophy, dispensed human reason from any need of initiative and forbade it, in any case, to set up an independent philosophy. Subjected in this way to the despotic authority of dogma, Christian thought produced nothing much beyond a "scholasticism", a sort of religious-cum-philosophical syncretism, until reason threw off the yoke of faith and succeeded at last in creating modern rationalism. Thus, Christian doctrine deflected or corrupted philosophical thought or, at the very least, it was an obstacle in its path, just as alchemy and astrology were fraudulent substitutes for chemistry and astronomy. The theory leaves no room for discussion on the question of "Christian philosophy". Philosophy could only develop side by side with Christianity, which did nothing but impede its progress [1].

Against the rationalist school and until recent years, Christian historians and critics defended an interpretation of the history of Christian thought which can be found in its broad outlines in the en-

[1] It would be easy to illustrate this brief account by innumerable examples gleaned from rationalist literature, on the subject of the history of Christian thought. As regards the history of medieval philosophy during the last century, we need only recall the works of B. Hauréau, F. Picavet, E. Renan, L. Rougier, S. Reinach, L. Gauthier, E. Bréhier and L. Brunschvicg in French literature alone; in English, G. G. COULTON, *Studies in Medieval Thought* (1940).

cyclical *Aeterni Patris* of Leo XIII. The main points
of view can be summarized in the following way.
Christian Revelation provided man with a number
of truths guaranteed by divine authority; these truths
were accepted by faith and transmitted to us by the
*magisterium* of the Church. Far from hindering the
development of the intellectual life, the Christian
faith was a source of science and wisdom. In using
her authority to combat heresy (in other words, error),
the Church rendered a great service to the cause of
truth; this she also did by protecting literature and
the sciences, by founding so many abbeys and schools,
and by fostering the development of the universities.
A gradual renewal of knowledge can be traced stage
by stage through the Christian era, at first in a rather
confused form, then in clearer outline. The distinction between philosophy and theology, a distinction
acknowledged in the High Middle Ages, was realized
in effect in the twelfth and especially in the thirteenth centuries. We can therefore distinguish, in the
history of medieval thought, a theological movement
and a philosophical movement. The latter reached its
full strength in the great systems of the thirteenth
century, above all in Thomism and Scotism. The
philosophy which evolved side by side with theology
in the Middle Ages was a work of pure reason, on
which Christian doctrine exercised no direct influence. The indirect influence of Christianity was felt
in two ways. On the positive side, faith stimulated
the desire for knowledge and the love of truth; on
the negative side, the *magisterium* of the Church
had a control over the results attained by philosophers
and forbade them to reach such conclusions as would
contradict the teachings of revelation. In these doc-

trinal interventions, prohibitions and condemnations, the religious authorities sometimes abused their power, but on the whole the Church's control was for the good of human thought, for it preserved it from grave errors and from many a formidable crisis. Except for a few isolated cases, this control was far less tyrannical than rationalist historians make out and it certainly did not hinder the development of western philosophy in any way. In short, Christian Revelation greatly enriched human thought and stimulated the intelligence. It called for a harmonious and beneficial collaboration between faith and reason, with the object of creating a complete system of knowledge, a really complete wisdom, consisting of theology, philosophy and the positive sciences. This general organization of knowledge was achieved in its main essentials by Albert the Great and Thomas Aquinas[1].

These views have been modified to a considerable extent by the works of M. Gilson. The interpretation of medieval thought proposed by M. Gilson seems to us to be an attempt to reconcile, at least in part, the thesis of the rationalist historians and that of the Christian historians. The latter, as we have just said, unanimously affirmed the existence in the Middle Ages of a philosophy in the strictest sense; they reduced the influence of Christianity on this philosophy to an action which was *indirect* and, in the last analysis, *accidental*, an action such as that which other non-philosophical factors bring to bear on the devel-

[1] Among those subscribing to this interpretation of the history of Christian thought, we might mention, besides Leo XIII in *Aeterni Patris*, F. Ehrle, Cl. Baeumker, P. Mandonnet, M. De Wulf, M. Grabmann, B. Geyer, D. J. B. Hawkins, S. J. Curtis, F. Copleston.

opment of any concrete thought whatsoever. M. Gilson does not apparently see things in quite the same way. He thinks he has found a new angle on the matter, which enables us to overcome to some extent the antagonism between Christian and rationalist historians. He affirms, with the Christians, that the medieval era possessed a real and very fruitful philosophical life of its own; with the rationalists, he recognizes the fact that the medieval philosophies were not philosophies in the current sense of the word, but systems elaborated under the influence of dogma, philosophies which were *specifically Christian*. Of course, there is still a radical difference between M. Gilson and the rationalist critics—for M. Gilson, the Christianity which inspired these philosophies was not a defect or obstacle, but the hidden reason for their power and fecundity [1].

This new outlook of M. Gilson's has furnished much of the material for the controversy on the problem of "Christian philosophy". It has given rise to an abundant literature and has been the occasion of several historical essays, all seeking to discover more precisely the nature and importance of the Christian factor in the formulation of Western thought, since the beginning of the Christian era.

There can be no question here of our taking up, *ex professo*, the examination and discussion of those pro-

---

[1] I have developed these ideas further in a communication to the Scholastic Congress held in Rome in 1950, entitled: *L'interprétation de la pensée médiévale au cours du siècle écoulé*. The text of this communication appeared in the Acts of the Congress (Rome, 1951), and also in the *Revue Philosophique de Louvain* (February, 1951).

blems of historical synthesis which are posed for us by the intellectual life of the thirteenth century. However, we shall have to choose what line we are to follow, in the light of the works enumerated above, and take sides in the controversies which still exist, concerning the general picture which is to be painted of the thirteenth century.

# CHAPTER IV

# THE INTRODUCTION OF ARISTOTLE
# INTO PARIS
## (1200-1230)

With the dawning of the thirteenth century, we have the starting-point of a new era, the beginning of the heyday of medieval Christianity. The triumph of the Papacy and Church, in the struggle between Priesthood and Empire, was fully achieved in the reign of Innocent III (1198-1216). The formation of distinctive nationalities and the strengthening of royal power in many countries of Europe favoured internal unity and peace. The capture of Constantinople by the crusaders in 1204 and the creation of a Latin Empire in the East brought the ancient centres of Hellenic and Hellenistic culture within reach of inquisitive Western minds. The communes and corporations, which were everywhere being formed, assured a material prosperity favourable to study. The scientific movement was accelerated by the foundation of the first universities, in Paris, Oxford, Bologna and Naples; while the spread of the mendicant orders helped to multiply the centres of study and to staff them with a numerous and active personnel. Finally, relations with the Arab world were further intensified and contacts were established between the Arabian and Latin cultures.

The thirteenth century was to provide medieval

Christianity with the decisive crisis of its development
in the field of the intellectual life. For the first time
Christian thinkers were to be confronted with Aristotle; his naturalistic view of the universe was to come
face to face with the Christian outlook so long familiar to the minds of men, thanks to the Church's
teaching. Latin theology, Augustinian in its inspiration, had without much difficulty found a place for
neo-Platonic speculations, which were in the direction of religious contemplation and the mystical life,
but there was a more suspicious air about Aristotle's
empiricism and it displayed more disturbing tendencies. Since the use of his logic in theology had
managed to stir up trouble for the religious world,
one might well expect even more violent upsets when
the whole of his philosophy was revealed. As Fr. Mandonnet puts it, "conceived as it was without any religious preoccupation whatsoever, it (Aristotle's philosophy) failed, despite its reservations and even its
reticence perhaps, to recognize some of those philosophical truths which the great monotheistic religions
placed at the foundation of their beliefs". Yet, for
all that, Aristotle was to be accepted by the Western
world, as he had been accepted by the Arabs, because
of the exceptional scientific qualities of his work, as
we have previously observed in agreement with Fr.
Mandonnet.

Already in the twelfth century, the great French
schools had been famed throughout Europe, and at
the end of the century Paris became the intellectual
metropolis of Christianity, at least where philosophical and theological studies were concerned. The different ideas so excitedly debated in the university of

Paris spread beyond its boundaries and came almost completely to dominate the intellectual life of Christian Europe in the thirteenth century. From now onwards, we shall concentrate on this privileged centre of study.

The penetration of Aristotelianism into the university of Paris raises a whole host of problems, which can be reckoned under four main heads. The first problem, which affects all the others, concerns the *translations* of Aristotle. What works of Aristotle were known in the thirteenth century ? When, where and by whom were they translated. What are these translations worth ? How far were they diffused ? Next, there comes the problem of the *legal situation* of Aristotle's works in Paris. What attitude towards Aristotelianism was adopted by the duly constituted authorities—the popes, bishops, councils and the university itself ? What place was given to Aristotle in the curricula ? A third problem is concerned with the *doctrinal influence* of Aristotle. When did it first make itself felt ? In what centres of study and through which masters ? Was this influence direct or indirect, and did it result from the reading of Aristotle's works or was it still exercised through intermediaries, such as Boethius, Abelard and the Arabs ? Was Aristotle understood ? Did they accept his ideas or react against them ? How important an influence was he by comparison with other doctrinal sources ? What is the best way of judging this influence ? Did it have fortunate or unfortunate consequences ? Finally, a problem closely connected with the preceding one concerns the existence of a *Latin Aristotelianism*. Were there in the thirteenth century one, or several, schools of philosophy claiming Aristotle as their master, and do they in fact deserve to be called Aristotelian ? What reservations and subtle shades of meaning are to be noted with respect to this designation ?

All these problems are connected and we shall not deal with them one by one. It is better, if we are to respect true historical perspectives, to trace the development of Aristotelianism, keeping close to the chronological succession of the relevant happenings.

In what way and in what stages was the philosophical emancipation of Christianity in the thirteenth century accomplished ?

The historians who have made a study of the doctrinal trends of the century have not always taken sufficient account of the concrete circumstances in which these trends found their origin and development. In our study we shall concentrate on the actual everyday life of the university of Paris; and we shall attempt to find out what in actual life were the reactions of the various centers of study composing the *studium generale* of Paris.

## *The new literature at the turn of the century*

Recent works on the Latin translations of Aristotle establish the fact that the greater part of his writings were available for Latin readers by 1200. The whole of his *Organon* had been translated; the *Logica Vetus* had been in circulation since Boethius, and the *Logica Nova* had come into general use during the twelfth century. A good part of the *Libri Naturales* had been translated from the Arabic by Gerard of Cremona (who died in 1187), namely the *Physics*, the *De Generatione*, the *De Caelo* and the first three books of

the *De Meteoris*. The fourth book of the *De Meteoris* and the *De Generatione* had been translated
from the Greek by Henricus Aristippus (died 1162).
Besides these, we owe to some unknown translators
of the twelfth century the translations from Greek to
Latin of the *Physics*, the *De Anima*, and the *Parva
Naturalia*. Part of the *Metaphysics* existed in Latin
(Books I to IV, chapter 4), and this first anonymous
fragment has been given the name *Metaphysica Ve-
tustissima* to distinguish it from later translations.
Finally, there existed in the twelfth century a partial
translation of the *Nicomachean Ethics*, which is also
anonymous. This fragment, comprising Books II and
III of Aristotle's work, will later be given the name
*Ethica Vetus*.

To these Aristotelian works, it is as well to add the
commentaries which helped to make them known:
the *Isagoge* of Porphyry (an introduction to the *Categories*), translated by Marius Victorinus and by
Boethius; the commentaries of Boethius on the *Categories* and on the *De Interpretatione*; the commentaries of Themistius on the Posterior Analytics; Alfarabi's *Distinctio super librum Aristotelis de Naturali
Auditu*; and finally the great paraphrase of Avicenna
which we shall deal with later.

We must here note that the work usually known as
the *Liber de Causis*, which was spuriously attributed
to Aristotle (it was in fact a commentary on theses
taken from the *Institutio Theologica* of Proclus), was
translated from Arabic into Latin by Gerard of Cremona (that is, before 1187) [1]. St. Thomas was the

---

[1] The author of this little treatise was probably the Arab
philosopher Alfarabi, who died in 949 or 950: cf. H. Bédoret,
*L'auteur et le traducteur du Liber de Causis* (1938).

first to realize the true origin of the treatise, thanks to William of Moerbeke's translation of the *Institutio Theologica*. Another work of Proclus, the *Elementatio Physica* or *De Motu*, was translated from Greek about 1160 by someone unknown.

Apart from these texts of Proclus, there were few direct sources of Platonism and neo-Platonism at the end of the twelfth century. Of Plato's works they had a fragment of the *Timaeus*, thanks to Cicero and Chalcidius, and the *Phaedo* and *Meno*, which had been translated about the middle of the twelfth century. This was all that the Middle Ages knew of Plato's writings, and they did not possess a single work of Plotinus. On the other hand there were many indirect sources of neo-Platonism: Latin neo-Platonists of antiquity such as Apuleius, Chalcidius and Macrobius; and the ecclesiastical writers, of whom we must mention, from the point of view of Platonic influence, especially Nemesius, Pseudo-Dionysius and St. Augustine. The *De Natura Hominis* of Nemesius, attributed to St. Gregory of Nyssa until the sixteenth century, had been translated as early as the eleventh century by Alfanus (died 1085), and was again translated by Burgundio of Pisa in 1159. Pseudo-Dionysius, who was venerated throughout the Middle Ages as the Areopagite, disciple of St. Paul, had been translated three times before the thirteenth century: first by Hilduin, between 828 and 835; then by John Scot Erigena about 860; and finally by John the Saracen, about 1167.

To complete our description of the philosophical library that was at the disposal of the Latin world by the end of the thirteenth century we must make mention of the Arab literature. Besides various writings on mathematics, astronomy, the natural sciences and medicine, translated during the eleventh and twelfth centuries, the Latin West had the translators of Toledo to thank for a series of important philosophical works. To the translations of Aristotle and of the *Liber de Causis* already noted, we must add the following: various writings of Alkindi, among others the *De Intellectu*; the *De Differentia inter Animam et Spiritum* of Costa ben Luca; the *De Scientiis*, the *De Ortu Scientiarum* and the *De Intellectu* of Alfarabi, besides his *Distinctio super librum Aristotelis de Naturali Auditu*; the *Liber Definitionum* and the *De Elementis* of the Jew Isaac Israeli; the *Fons Vitae* of the Jew Avicebron; finally and above all, considerable portions of Avicenna's great philosophical encyclopaedia, known in Arabic as *Aš-Sifa* (*Book of Healing*) and known to the Latin World under the name of *Sufficientia*. This encyclopaedia, being a paraphrase of Aristotle, contributed largely to the spread of his doctrines in the twelfth century.

In short, those masters of the university of Paris who were interested in philosophy at the turn of the century were already in possession of a very respectable amount of literary material. Among these sources, the works of Aristotle, accompanied by the Greek, Latin and Arabic commentaries on them, were the most imposing. From this time onwards, his logic was the universal instrument of knowledge, while his other doctrines were gradually infiltrating, especially through the channel of Avicenna. Neo-Platonism was the only serious rival of Aristotelianism in the field of philosophy, and, though there were few direct sources of Greek neo-Platonism, there was nevertheless the very effective influence of the metaphysics of

Plotinus, transmitted by Pseudo-Dionysius, St. Augustine, Avicebron and Avicenna, to mention only the principal intermediaries. In the more general field of religious and moral ideas, first place must be given to the intellectual influence of Christianity, the doctrine of which was set out in concrete form in the writings of the Fathers and theologians.

### The ban on Aristotle: the first prohibitions

We know very little about the beginnings of Aristotelianism in Paris, for they are still wreathed in obscurity. This fact is easily enough explained. As we have already said, it was not usual for anyone to make a career of the Arts Faculty—*non est consenescendum in artibus*—but only to teach there for a few years before going on to further studies. As a result the members of the Arts Faculty wrote very little, and what literature they did produce was rather immature. More often than not, all that we have of theirs is notes from their oral teaching. Thus, when printing was invented a large number of theological works had the honour of going to press but philosophical literature was almost entirely neglected. In recent years some light has already been thrown on the first years of Aristotelianism by an increasingly methodical employment of manuscript material.

The events of 1210 and 1215 show that the academic circles in Paris did not remain indifferent to the new philosophical literature. The university of Paris, that is, the Parisian corporation of men of study (*universitas magistrorum et scolarium parisius studentium*), came into being about 1200, being formed from the existing cathedral schools. The year 1200 can be considered the date of its legal constitution, because in that year, by the "charter" of Philip Augustus, the masters and students of Paris were released from the ordinary jurisdiction and entrusted to the sole jurisdiction of the bishop and chancellor of Paris. Ten years later, in 1210, the enactments of the Council of Paris reveal how far the interest in philosophy had increased during the preceding years. The late Mgr. Grabmann traced the ecclesiastical interventions concerning Aristotle between 1210 and 1231, and has cast all the light which could be desired on the subject: we need only to follow the eminent historian in our outline of the events [1].

The Council of Paris, held in 1210, at which all the bishops of the ecclesiastical province of Sens were present, was presided over by Peter of Corbeil, Archbishop of Sens. The decrees of this synod first of all condemned Amalric of Bene and David of Dinant, as well as those clerics in Paris who had subscribed to their heresies. They then ordered that the "*quaternuli*" of David of Dinant (that is, as far as we know, the notebooks containing his works) should be handed over to the bishop before Christmas, in order to be burned. The text of the decrees continues as follows: "*nec libri Aristotelis de naturali philosophia nec commenta legantur Parisius publice vel secreto et hoc sub pena excommunicationis inhibemus*".

This text must be interpreted in the light of the corresponding text of 1215 which is a part of the statute promulgated in that year by Robert of Courçon. The latter had been professor of theology at

[1] M. GRABMANN, *I divieti ecclesiastici di Aristotele sotto Innocenzo III e Gregorio IX* (1941).

Paris, probably from 1204 to 1210. He was a boyhood friend of Pope Innocent III and became a cardinal in 1212. In 1215, he was given the task, as papal legate, of reorganizing the studies at Paris; the new statutes of the university were published under his direction in August, 1215. Among the rules laid down for the Faculty of Arts was contained the following in the matter of teaching: "*Et quod legant libros Aristotelis de dialectica tam de veteri quam de nova in scolis ordinarie et non ad cursum. Legant etiam in scolis ordinarie duos Priscianos vel alterum ad minus. Non legant in festivis diebus nisi philosophos et rhetoricas, et quadruvialia, et barbarismum, et ethicam, si placet, et quartum topichorum. Non legantur libri Aristotelis de metaphisica et de naturali philosophia nec summe de eisdem, aut de doctrina magistri David de Dinant, aut Amalrici heretici, aut Mauricii hyspani.*"

These two parallel texts raise a great number of problems, over which historians racked their brains for a long time. However, most of the problems can be considered solved today. We can accept the wise conclusions reached by Mgr. Grabmann in the work mentioned above, in which he takes account of all the known sources and all works on the subject.

It is obvious that the Council of Paris was mainly concerned with putting an end to the development of subversive ideas provoked by the teaching of Amalric of Bene. Amalric, who had been a master, first in arts, then in theology, died some years before the council met, but he had gained many adherents and his influence continued to be actively felt in the university. It is not easy to give an exact account of the nature of his doctrine and, as a result of this, it is difficult to determine his sources. It cannot be proved as yet that his errors have as their root the *libri naturales* of Aristotle or the Arabian commentaries on these books.

The Council of Paris next condemned David of Dinant. In this case the position is quite different, because David of Dinant's dependence on the *Physics* and *Metaphysics* of Aristotle has been firmly established by Fr. Théry, with the aid of numerous extracts from the *De Tomis* of the condemned philosopher, quoted by Albert the Great. This fact also explains the violence of Albert's attack, for he reproached David with having polluted Aristotle's philosophy with his own crude pantheistic and materialistic ideas.

To forbid the reading of the books of Aristotle was then a prudent protective measure, provoked by the way in which David of Dinant, and perhaps others with him, had made an improper use of the writings. Furthermore, a text from Roger Bacon gives us to understand that provision was made, in the 1210 prohibition, for the errors of Aristotle which concerned the eternity of the world and of time, and also his ideas on divination by dreams.

It is certain that the decree was intended to include some writings of Aristotle himself. It is also very probable that we should take the expression "*libri de naturali philosophia*" to mean all books dealing with "natural philosophy" as opposed to "rational philosophy" and "moral philosophy". The *Metaphysics* was therefore included among the prohibited books, and the statute of 1215, when it expressly named the work, did nothing more than render the decree of 1210 more explicit. The "*commenta*", mentioned in 1210 and the "*summae*", forbidden in 1215, were

Avicenna's paraphrases (and perhaps the works of Alfarabi also) for, as we already know, a fair part of Avicenna's philosophical encyclopaedia had been translated in the twelfth century. The Council of 1210 might very well give it the name of *"commenta"*, since it was in reality a paraphrase of Aristotle; and Robert of Courçon was able to use the word *"summae"* because of Avicenna's method, which was so often to make a synthetic summary of Aristotle's text. Moreover, the Arabic text calls the sections of Avicenna's encyclopaedia *"Kullun"*, which means *"summae"*. Fr. Mandonnet thought the *"summae de eisdem"* were extracts from, or summaries of, the prohibited books, composed by the masters of Paris after 1210 so that they could continue teaching Aristotle, while respecting the letter of the decree. This hypothesis does not seem acceptable, for it lacks any historical foundation. We do possess numerous summaries (*abbreviationes, summulae, compendia, epitomata*) of the works of Aristotle, but none of those on natural philosophy goes back to the period of the Council.

The term *"legantur"* should be understood in the technical sense which was current in the thirteenth century. The council and the legate forbade the *teaching* of the *libri naturales*, that is, the works could not be used as text-books for the lessons of the faculty. A master would incur excommunication even if the lessons he organized were private or secret (*secreto*). On the other hand, to read or use the books personally was still allowed. We must add that the double prohibition of 1210 and 1215 was a strictly local affair, applicable to no centre of study except the university of Paris. Thus, we find the university of Toulouse issuing an advertising circular in 1229, with the object of attracting students and masters to the university, and this publication stresses the fact that the books of Aristotle, forbidden in Paris, can be expounded at Toulouse. The official texts of the prohibitions do not mention any time limit and later events show that the provisions made in 1210 and 1215 were still in force in 1229 and 1231; we must therefore consider as inexact, indications given by the chroniclers Robert of Auxerre and Caesar of Heisterbach, according to which the prohibition of 1210 was pronounced for three years only.

Robert of Courçon's statute also declared that books or summaries containing the doctrines of David of Dinant, the heretic Amalric or Maurice the Spaniard, should not be expounded. Historians have for a long time been curious about the last-named. Some have wished to identify him with Averroes (e.g. Renan, Bardenhewer, Mandonnet, de Vaux), others with Dominic Gundisalvi, Avicebron, Avicenna or Maurice Bourdin, Archbishop of Braga; while M. Asin Palacios prefers to take him as an unknown Spanish Moslem. Following Mgr. Grabmann's example, the best we can do here is to reproduce the conclusion of the excellent study made by Fr. Bouyges: "While we still await information, we should see the *Mauricius hyspanus* mentioned in the 1215 decree of Robert of Courçon as Mauricius hyspanus and nothing more".

Fr. Mandonnet thought the word "Mauricii" was a corruption of "Mauri"; it therefore followed that we should read "of the Spanish Moor" and not "of Maurice the Spaniard". This Moor would be Averroes, the philosopher of Cordova. Fr. Bouyges, in agreement with many other historians, has shown up the weak

points in Fr. Mandonnet's interpretation. Its chief
fault lies in the fact that it is founded on a gratuitous
hypothesis, for no document gives us grounds for
saying that Averroes was called "the Spanish Moor".
It must nevertheless be recognized that the hypothesis
is by no means unreasonable and it therefore deserves
to be retained, provided it is put forward in an acceptable form. Averroes died in 1198 but his literary
activity and therefore his renown must obviously be
given an earlier date. Thus, from before the end of
the twelfth century he must have been known among
Christians in Toledo as the author of important commentaries on the writings of Aristotle. Taking this
into consideration, it seems quite possible that Robert
of Courçon had in his possession some document,
coming for example from Spain, which was known
in Paris and which made much of the commentaries
of a famous "Spanish Moor", *"alicuius mauri hyspani"*.
Reading the word *"mauri"* as a badly written or
abridged form of *"mauricii"*, the legate would then
think it prudent, as a precautionary measure, to pro-
hibit in advance the Arab philosopher's commentaries
thus discovered. All this is of course mere conjecture—
we only put the hypothesis forward in order to show
that the mention of Averroes in the statute of 1215
would not imply the existence of Latin translations
of his writings at that date.

Mgr. Grabmann thought that the Faculty of Theology in Paris had something to do with the measures
taken by the council and legate, in 1210 and 1215
respectively, against the books of Aristotle. In the introduction to the new statute of 1215, Robert of Courçon mentions the support which he has sought from
prudent counsellors: *"nos de bonorum virorum con-*

*silio scolarum tranquillitati volentes in posterum pro-
videre, ordinavimus et statuimus in hunc modum"*;
all the indications are that he means the masters of the
Faculty of Theology.

As we have noted above, the theological school of
Paris showed extremely conservative tendencies at the
end of the twelfth century, besides a marked preference for Holy Scripture and moral and pastoral theology, while adopting a suspicious attitude towards
logic and profane studies. The Archbishop of Sens,
Peter of Corbeil, had himself been professor of theology at Paris, from 1190 to 1198 (liturgy and exegesis being his particular subjects). The legate Robert
of Courçon had also been a *magister regens in theolo-
gia*[1] at Paris, probably from 1204 to 1210. His *Summa theologica*, preserved for us in numerous manuscripts, enables us to define him pretty accurately as
a member of the group of conservative theologians,
which concentrated chiefly on practical problems.
Like master Peter the Cantor, Robert saw theology as
a *caelestis philosophia*, an expression that reminds us
of the Augustinian notion of philosophy. He also
shows himself to be in the Augustinian line when he
stresses the conformity which should exist between
the sublime nature of the theologian's teaching and
the holiness of his life. He writes in his *Summa*: *"Qui
legit publice sacram scripturam iter maioris perfec-
tionis arripuit quam aliquis Clarevallensis"*. In short,
the papal legate, like the Archbishop of Sens, was
very closely acquainted with the schools of Paris,

[1] Students at a university who did not proceed to an academic career after taking their degrees were known as *magistri
non regentes*; one who went on to teach after qualifying was
called *magister regens*.

which he had not so very long left, and he must have
felt quite at home among his old colleagues of the Theological Faculty, whose spirit he understood and shared.

These men had long been suspicious of logic, and
their suspicion was quickly changed into apprehen-
sion and anger when the young and turbulent members of the Arts Faculty started reading the newly
introduced works of Aristotle. The young men, already smitten with an insane love of profane knowledge, went crazy over the "new philosophy". They
welcomed the most subversive ideas of a David of
Dinant or of an Amalric of Bene; they had the intolerable audacity to oppose the wisdom of pagan philosophers to the Christian wisdom of the theologians;
in fact, the whole outlook which pervaded the events
of 1210 and 1215 explains the reaction which, from
before 1210, showed itself in the sermons of Prevostin of Cremona, who was Chancellor of the university of Paris from 1206 until his death (in the
year 1210, or a little after). These sermons severely
censured the "vain wisdom" cultivated by logicians
and the lovers of "useless subtleties" in the "philosophical faculties". Theologians were warned against introducing philosophy into the study of Holy Scripture: *"odibiles Deo erimus, strepitum ranarum Egyp-
tii in terra Gessen traducere molientes"*. In his *Summa theologiae* Prevostin did not conceal his anger at
the *"logomachia"* which reigned in the Arts Faculty.

Taking all this into account, it seems that the prohibitions of Aristotle's natural philosophy, in 1210
and in 1215, were inspired by the Theological Faculty of Paris; we must see them as defensive measures, aimed at protecting theology from the pagan
infiltrations of the new Aristotle.

Finally, Mgr. Grabmann reminds us that Robert of
Courçon was acting under the special commands of
Innocent III, who had studied at Bologna and at
Paris, where he had been the pupil of Peter the Cantor and the fellow-student of his future legate. His
theological writings have the same characteristics as
those of his master in Paris and of the conservative
group to which the latter belonged. It is not impossible
therefore that the measures taken against pagan philosophy by Robert of Courçon corresponded to the
personal ideas of Pope Innocent. The pope's preoccupation was to safeguard the purity of the faith
and his whole pontificate was one long struggle
against heresy.

The events of 1210 and 1215 are almost the only
point on which much is known in the history of
Aristotelianism in Paris, from 1210 until 1230. The
documents relating to the teaching or the literary
activity of the masters of arts during this period are
almost non-existent. It is not certain that David of
Dinant taught in Paris; Amalric of Bene was master
in the Arts Faculty before teaching theology but,
as we have said, little is known about his ideas. Jordan
of Saxony, who entered the Order of Preachers in
1220 and two years later succeeded St. Dominic as
head of the order, had taught in the Arts Faculty
round about the time of the prohibitions of Aristotle.
But his main subject was grammar and, if he is to be
identified with Jordan the Forester (*Jordanus Ne-
morarius*), mathematics also. Mgr. Grabmann has
managed to unearth a number of important writings
on logic which belong to the end of the twelfth
century and the first half of the thirteenth century,
but almost all these writings are anonymous and only

very approximately dated. As regards the first use made of Aristotle's *Metaphysics* and *Libri naturales* in the Arts Faculty of Paris, we possess no direct information at the present time, unless the *De Finibus Rerum Naturalium* of Arnold of Saxony is a product of the faculty [1].

The little work entitled *Disciplina scholarium* throws some light on the Faculty of Arts prior to 1230. It was composed around 1230, probably by an English student, Elias of Trickingham, who received his education in Paris. In the work, he acquaints us with his scholastic and pedagogical experiences. He gives us, through the mouth of Boethius, a description of the organisation of studies in the Arts Faculty of Paris. He mentions only Aristotle's writings on Logic. Later, this pseudo-Boethius was often commented on.

Taking all things into account, the prohibitions of 1210 and 1215 throw some light on the period which immediately preceded them, a period which witnessed the first penetration of Aristotelianism into Paris [2]. But they also tell us something of the succeeding years, in that they explain why, during the first half of the century, the study of Aristotle's treatises on physics and metaphysics seems in Paris to have been paralysed, or neglected in favour of logic and ethics.

---

[1] The *De Finibus* (or better *De Virtutibus*) *Rerum Naturalium* of Arnold of Saxony was composed between 1220 and 1230; it reflects in a very interesting manner the philosophical curiosity of the period.

[2] The chronicler Robert of Auxerre, speaking of the events of 1210, sums up the situation as follows: "*Librorum quoque Aristotelis, qui de naturali phylosophya inscripti sunt, et ante paucos annos Parisius ceperant lectitari, interdicta est lectio, quia ex ipsis errorum semina viderentur exorta*". Other chronicles speak in similar fashion.

We should remember, however, that Aristotle's *realis philosophia* was being studied avidly elsewhere during this same period, especially in England. The situation in Paris was the normal consequence of the measures taken there at the beginning of the century.

In conclusion, we can say that one fact dominates our inquiry into the events of 1210 and 1215: from that time on, there existed a conflict between the Faculty of Arts and the Faculty of Theology. As we shall later discover, this conflict grew less after 1230 and almost completely died out, only to blaze up even more fiercely after 1260, reaching its highest point at the great condemnation of Aristotle in 1277.

While the schools of Paris were feeling the first upheavals caused by the introduction of Aristotle and the pagan philosophers, other persons of a different kind were preparing to make their entry into the city, bringing a new spirit to the place: we mean, of course, the Mendicant Friars. The order of St. Dominic had been canonically instituted by a bull of Honorius III, dated the 22nd December 1216. Some months later, on the 12th September 1217, the first of the Dominicans arrived in Paris. In August 1218, they took possession of the house of Saint-Jacques; and when St. Dominic visited the new friary in the spring of 1219, he found thirty or more brothers already in residence. In the same year, the first Friars Minor passed through the gates of Paris. Both the Dominicans and the Franciscans immediately made numerous recruits in the schools, not only among the students, but among the masters also. This rapid development explains the part which they were soon to play in the teaching of theology.

## A *university on strike*

A second stage in the history of thirteenth century Aristotelianism is marked by the succession of events from 1228 to 1231.

On the 7th July 1228, Pope Gregory IX addressed a letter, crammed with biblical images, to the Theological Faculty in Paris, in which he warned theologians to be on their guard against a wrong use of philosophy and to remember that theology was a science whose principles were received by faith and were above the level of human reasoning. He claimed that philosophy was the servant of theology and theology was the queen of sciences. These positions were not to be reversed—the sovereign was not to be placed under the authority of the servant.

The content of this letter is vague, but it casts enough light on the development of the Faculty of Theology since 1215, especially if we compare its text with a series of theological documents of the same period. This is what Mgr. Grabmann has done, with the aid of university writings and sermons which reflect the same preoccupations as those of the pope.

Gregory IX had studied theology in Paris and, like Innocent III, had been the pupil of Peter the Cantor. He was a canonist and theologian, and was also favourable to letters and to the sciences. In the document of the 7th July 1228, he betrayed the anxiety which he felt at the sight of "profane novelties" gaining a larger place in the teaching of theology. We must conclude that, despite the measures taken in 1210 and 1215, a new trend of ideas had taken root in the Faculty of Theology, side by side with the old conservative outlook, which wished to remain faithful to the scriptural and patristic method. The new trend was doubtless kept alive by the Faculty's young recruits, who had made contact with the new philosophy when they were members of the Arts Faculty, and were now allowing the speculative method to fill a more and more important role in their theology. If their opponents are to be believed, these innovators were using philosophical terms and notions in the interpretation of the mysteries of the faith, without paying attention to the special nature of theological science or of knowledge through faith.

Among the documents which echo the admonitions of Gregory IX, it is interesting to note a passage from the *Sermo ad scholares*, delivered by Cardinal James of Vitry, because here we find Plato and Aristotle covered by the same censure: "*Ex philosophis autem quaedam possumus assumere ad commodum causae nostrae. Boethius quidem, de consolatione, totus catholicus est et moralis. Alii autem multa falsa et vana dixerunt, sicut Plato, qui planetas deos asseruit, et Aristoteles, qui mundum aeternum fuisse dogmatizavit. Unde in libris, quos naturales appellant, valde cavendum est, ne ex nimia inquisitione erremus ... Quum igitur libri theologici christiano possunt sufficere, non expedit in libris naturalibus nimis occupari.*" This document is certainly dealing with the conflict between the Christian spirit and pagan naturalism, and not with the rivalry between two philosophies, that of St. Augustine and that of Aristotle.

The first constitutions of the Order of Friars Preachers, drawn up by St. Raymond of Pennafort in the same year 1228, betray an outlook similar to that which we have just discovered in the Theological Faculty of Paris. The Order was founded to preach and teach theology and we therefore find that the religious are ordered to concentrate on theological studies, to the exclusion of profane subjects. They may, however, consult the works of pagans and philosophers, so long as they do not spend too long on them. Only those who have obtained a dispensation may study the profane sciences and the liberal arts. The regulations are very concerned over two points which are quite opposed to each other. The rule which all are expected to follow reiterates a traditional idea, namely that all religious, who have vowed to serve God, should concern themselves only with the things of God, renouncing all vain curiosity and all the dissipation that comes from contact with profane knowledge. The apostolic ideal of the Dominicans did not modify this notion (or at least, not at first sight), since the object of their preaching also was the gospel message. However, the exceptions to the rule, allowed by the text of the constitutions, show that the legislators had something in mind quite different from this first idea. They saw how useful the profane sciences could be to theology, and realized that the study of those sciences could not be forbidden altogether. They also appreciated the fact that if they were to preach in intellectual circles and to fight heresies, they would need a solid training, in which philosophy and the liberal arts would be indispensable subjects. As we shall soon see, once they had made these first concessions, more and more were forced on them by the pressure of events, and the time was fast approaching when the Dominicans and the Franciscans would rival each other in their zeal for new conquests in knowledge, despite the scruples which persisted among some of them.

In Paris, friction was frequently caused between the turbulent inmates of the schools and the towns-folk. On Shrove Tuesday in 1229, there broke out a conflict which soon became extremely violent. It all started with a quarrel between a group of students and an innkeeper and, after many tragic mishaps, it resulted in the suspension of the course of studies and a general strike among the masters, who had sided with their students[1]. It was not long before the clerics began to leave for the provincial towns or for their native countries. The Pope took an active part in the affair. William of Auvergne had been named Bishop of Paris in 1228 and had received the orders of priesthood and episcopate in Rome itself. On the 23rd November 1229, Gregory IX sent him a letter in which he expressed regret at having elected him (*Penitet hunc hominem nos fecisse !*) and bitterly rebuked him for his idleness during the period of very grave crisis through which the university was passing. The Pope multiplied his proceedings and consultations until he thought that the ground had been well enough prepared for him to solve the conflict by direct intervention. This he did in his letter of the

[1] The decree of March 27th, 1229, published by the twenty-one provisors of the university, suspended all teaching for a period of six years! It forbade anyone to reside in the city or diocese of Paris for reasons of study. However, we know from other evidence that this decree was not fully observed. In the autumn of 1229, Roland of Cremona inaugurated his chair of theology, and in 1254 the secular masters were to complain bitterly that the Dominicans had taken advantage of the situation to establish themselves in the university: "*in illa paucitate scolarium que remansit Parisius*" (H. DENIFLE, *Chartularium...*, I, p. 253). The many university sermons dated 1230 and 1231 prove that a student body existed in Paris during those years.

13<sup>th</sup> April 1231, addressed to the professors and students of the university. This supremely important document (*Parens scientiarum Parisius*), which Mgr. Grabmann, like Mgr. Masnovo, called the *"Magna Charta"* of the university of Paris, contains some provisions important to our subject and we shall return to it in a few minutes.

At the very moment when the 1229 crisis had come to a head in Paris, the university of Toulouse was being born, as a result of the treaty concluded on Holy Thursday, 2<sup>nd</sup> April, 1229, between the young King Louis IX and Count Raymond VII of Toulouse, to put an end to the Albigensian war. Taking advantage of the strike at the university of Paris, the directors of the new university towards the end of 1229 addressed a propaganda circular to masters and students *"ubicumque terrarum studentibus"*, in which they boasted of the scientific merits of the new *studium generale* and promised the maximum liberty to the students. Among the academic advantages which they held up as an enticement before the eyes of men of letters, there is one which is of particular interest to us: *"Libros naturales, qui fuerant Parisius prohibiti, poterunt illic audire qui volunt nature sinum medullitus perscrutari"*. As we said earlier, this text clearly proves that the prohibitions of 1210 and 1215 were local affairs. But it also reveals that Cardinal Romano, who was papal legate in France and grand protector of the new university of Toulouse, had much broader views on the subject of Aristotle than many people still had in certain Parisian circles. He probably realized that Aristotelianism might well be assimilated by Christian thinkers and corrected where necessary. It is also probable that the Cardinal legate had a hand in the new measures taken by Gregory IX in 1231.

The first Dominicans, who had settled in Paris in 1217, had followed the lessons of master John of Barastre, their benefactor, and had managed to gain their degrees in theology. In 1229, during the strike, the Bishop of Paris bestowed a university chair on Roland of Cremona, who had become a master in May of the same year. Roland thus became the first holder of the first Dominican chair. He taught for only one year in Paris and was replaced in 1230 by his pupil Hugh of St. Cher, who taught from 1230 till 1235. On the 22nd September 1230, a secular master, John of St. Giles, took the Dominican habit at the house in Paris. He kept his chair and this therefore became the second Dominican chair in the Theological Faculty. His successor was Guerric of St. Quentin, who was *magister regens* from 1233 to 1242. This new situation, though accepted by Philip, the Chancellor, was later to arouse a lively opposition on the part of the secular masters, especially after 1252, and they did not become fully resigned to it until 1259.

The Franciscans obtained a chair of theology in Paris by the same means, that is, by the entry into the Order of Alexander of Hales, who had been a secular master, probably since 1226. He became a Franciscan about 1236, and carried on teaching until 1238 or 1241. He was succeeded by his pupil, John of la Rochelle, who occupied the chair until his death on the 8th February 1245.

It is not difficult to understand the importance of this incorporation of the mendicant orders into the Faculty of Theology. The Friars were henceforth to play an active part in university life and to figure largely in all the struggles of every kind which were to stir up trouble in the schools of Paris. From now on in fact, the part they were to play in the history of Aristotelianism in Paris would be of the greatest importance.

We can now return to the letter of the 13<sup>th</sup> April 1231, by which Gregory IX restored peace and order to the university. The passage which interests us concerns the teaching of philosophy and theology: "*Ad hec iubemus ut magistri artium unam lectionem de Prisciano et unum post alium ordinarie semper legant, et libris illis naturalibus, qui in Concilio provinciali ex certa causa prohibiti fuere, Parisius non utantur, quousque examinati fuerint et ab omni errorum suspitione purgati. Magistri vero et scolares theologie in facultate quam profitentur se studeant laudabiliter exercere, nec philosophos se ostentent, sed satagant fieri theodocti, nec loquantur in lingua populi et populi linguam hebream cum Azotica confundentes, sed de illis tantum in scolis questionibus disputent, que per libros theologicos et sanctorum patrum tractatus valeant terminari.*"

This text calls for a brief commentary, for which we shall rely on those of Mgr. Masnovo and Mgr. Grabmann. When we compare the letter of 1231 with that of 1228, we find that there has been a change in tone: the ban of 1210 on Aristotle is maintained, but only provisionally, until the *libri naturales* have been examined. The Pope does not say that they will be purged of the errors that they contain, but of every *suspicion* of error which anyone might have of them. The directives to theologians are inspired by methodological considerations, rather than by any wish to ward off a doctrinal danger. The Pope exhorts theologians not to play the philosopher, but to respect the proper nature of theology and to take their guidance from the traditional sources of the sacred science. The directive concerning the teaching of Priscian's *Institutiones grammaticales* will also be noted. It is probable that the Arts Faculty had tended to neglect grammar in favour of philosophy, whereas the theologians attached great importance to grammar and to linguistic logic (or speculative grammar), because of the constant use which was made of these subjects in theology, notably in the chapter on the divine names (*De divinis nominibus*).

Ten days later, by a letter dated the 23rd April 1231, Gregory IX set up a commission of three members for the examination of Aristotle's *libri naturales*. After a preamble in which he reminds us that the Hebrews must enrich themselves with the spoils of the Egyptians, the pope continues in the following terms: "*Ceterum cum, sicut intelleximus, libri naturalium, qui Parisius in Concilio provinciali fuere prohibiti, quedam utilia et inutilia continere dicantur, ne utile per inutile vitietur, discretioni vestre, de qua plenam in Domino fiduciam obtinemus, per apostolica scripta sub obtestatione divini judicii firmiter precipiendo mandamus, quatinus libros ipsos examinantes sicut convenit subtiliter et prudenter, que ibi erronea seu scandali vel offendiculi legentibus inveneritis illativa, penitus resecetis, ut que sunt suspecta remotis, incunctanter ac inoffense in reliquis studeatur.*"

It seems then, that Gregory IX had been won over to the idea that the study of Aristotle could be of some profit to Christian knowledge. In this text, he ordered that a profound examination should be made, expressing his desire in terms which stressed the grave responsibility of the members of the commission. He seems to have had in mind a work of dissection, which would consist in expurgating the works of Aristotle of all dangerous or suspect passages (*penitus resecetis, que sunt suspecta remotis*) ; but he doubtless left the choice of a working method to the scholars whom he had chosen and in whom he had every confidence. On this point, Mgr. Grabmann observed that various quite practical methods of procedure could have been adopted, and in fact, such methods had been used for other writings, as many manuscripts testify. For example, they could have made out a list of Aristotle's errors and affixed it to each copy of his works; or they could have marked the heretical and dangerous passages with a marginal sign; or they might even have crossed out these passages in already existing copies and omitted them in later copies.

Of the three members of the commission, the second, Simon of Authie (*Simon de Alteis*), is known only as a canon of Amiens; nothing is known of his literary or professorial activity. On the contrary, the other two are interesting personalities in the university world. The first one to be named, who was probably the president of the commission, is William of Auxerre, Archdeacon of Beauvais. William had already been a professor of theology in Paris for many years. In April and May of 1230, he journeyed to Rome on behalf of King Louis IX, and here he had been the confidant of Gregory IX, who had sought his advice before setting the affairs of the university in order. It was therefore quite natural that the pope should think of him for the delicate mission with which we are now dealing. Moreover, the archdeacon had the necessary qualities for carrying out this difficult task. He was of an even temperament and peaceful in character and, as a theologian of high repute, he had made contact with the new Aristotelian philosophy, without renouncing the traditional tendencies of the theological school of Paris. The third member of the commission was Stephen of Provins, a canon of Rheims and later of Paris, who was famous for his personal relations with Michael Scot, the translator of Averroes. (In 1227, Michael Scot dedicated to Stephen his translation of the *De Caelo* of Aristotle, with the commentary of Averroes.) Basing his conclusions on the researches of Fr. de Vaux and M. Haskins, Mgr.Grabmann thought that Stephen taught in the Faculty of Arts and was the commission's real specialist on Aristotelianism, whereas William of Auxerre was there to represent the interests of theology.

We have no information on the activity of the commission charged with the correction of Aristotle, nor do we know anything of the results of their work. It is probable that the initiative taken by Gregory IX was checked by various difficulties when his ideas were actually put to the test. As Fr. Mandonnet observes, "apart from the fact that it would have been difficult to make men whose philosophical curiosity had been strongly aroused accept a mutilated text, there would remain the insurmountable problem of censoring the treatises of Aristotle, which are so concise". Fr. de Vaux thinks that the recent translation of the commentaries of Averroes, and their introduction into Paris soon after 1230, hastened the failure of the commission, by showing its members that their undertaking could not be brought to completion. Perhaps the most natural reason for the cessation of work was the fact that its director, William of Auxerre, died at Rome on the 3rd November, 1231. Be that as it may, Aristotle was not corrected, for on the 22nd September, 1245, Innocent IV extended the ban on Aristotle's *libri naturales* to Toulouse, using the same words as those used by Gregory IX in 1231: *"Libris illis naturalibus qui in Concilio provinciali ex certa causa prohibiti fuere, non utantur omnino Tolose, quousque examinati fuerint, et ab omni errorum suspicione purgati."*

The attempt made by Gregory IX to facilitate the assimilation of Aristotelianism bears witness to the foresight of this great pope and to his devotion both to the cause of knowledge and to the cause of the university of Paris. This is a fact which Hauréau was only too pleased to stress. This author even regarded the letter of the 23rd April 1231 as an abrogation of the decrees of 1210 and 1215, but this is an obvious exaggeration.

# CHAPTER V

# THE GROWTH
# OF ARISTOTELIANISM AT PARIS
## (1230-1250)

We can draw a fairly accurate picture of the Paris schools between 1230 and 1250, thanks to literary evidence which is relatively abundant, at least by comparison with the extreme penury of the preceding period. But before attempting to reconstruct the philosophical life of these years we must mention the progress made in the field of translation during the period.

## New wave of translations

The researches of Fr. de Vaux have given a new turn to the problem of the introduction of Averroes into the Christian world. Until about 1930 it was commonly thought that the penetration of Averroes dated from the first years of the thirteenth century, and he was thought to have played some part in the events of 1210 and 1215. We have said above that the *commenta* referred to by the Council of Paris must have been those of Avicenna and perhaps those of Alfarabi, but not those of Averroes. As for the famous *Mauricius Hyspanus* mentioned in the decree of Robert of

Courçon, we have shown that even if one is inclined
to identify him with Averroes, the legate's wording
does not necessarily involve the existence of Latin
writings of Averroes at this date.

Now there are decisive indications that Averroes
was not known in Christian circles before 1230. The
first quotations of Averroes are to be seen in the *De
Universo* and the *De Anima* of William of Auvergne.
These works were composed most probably between
1231 and 1236; and the way in which the bishop of
Paris speaks of Averroes shows that he had very little
knowledge of him—he has no suspicion that Averroes's work holds any danger for Christian thought.
Philip the Chancellor is the next witness to the existence of a Latin Averroes. In his *Summa de Bono*,
written between 1228 and 1236, he cites Averroes's
*Metaphysics* once, and his *Tractatus de Anima* once.
Some years later, Albert the Great's *Summa de Creaturis,* composed around 1240, has about 80 references
to Averroes in the first two parts. The references are to
the *Metaphysics*, the *De Anima*, the *De Caelo*, an ex-
tract from *De Animalibus,* and the *De Substantia Orbis*. The *Summa de Creaturis* also shows some knowledge of the paraphrase on the *Parva Naturalia,* but
attributes it to Alfarabi. On the other hand, Albert
does not quote the *Physics*, the *De Generatione*, or the
*De Meteoris*.

As regards the origin and date of the versions, Fr.
de Vaux reaches conclusions which he himself divides
into two categories. The following facts are *certain*:
that Michael Scot translated the *De Caelo* of Averroes after 1217; that he worked at his translations
while he was at the court of Frederick II, king of
Sicily, between 1228 and 1235; that shortly after

1230 the latter sent some new translations to the Italian universities; and that about the same time translations of Averroes were introduced into Paris. In addition to this, it is *probable* that the first serious attempt to translate Averroes took place at the court of Frederick II between 1227 and 1230; that Michael Scot played a major part in this enterprise; that he translated there in particular the *De Caelo*; that these translations were included in those sent to Italy by Frederick II; and that they arrived in Paris shortly afterwards.

Apart from the *De Caelo* and the *De Anima*, it is difficult to determine which translations of Averroes are the work of Michael Scot himself. He may be the translator of the *De Generatione*, of book IV of the *De Meteoris*, the *Parva Naturalia*, and the little treatise *De Substantia Orbis*.

Fr. de Vaux tries to prove that Michael probably did not translate Averroes between 1220 and 1227; but we must admit that his arguments do not seem very solid. "Such an undertaking", he says, "would suppose conditions which were difficult to realize". Manuscripts were necessary and the help of an interpreter. "Manuscripts and interpreters suppose a whole Jewish-Arab milieu, such as was by no means everywhere to be found". This is doubtless true; but we are dealing with a translator who had lived in Toledo, who could have obtained copies of Averroes and the services of a Jewish *socius* there; and if some motive of which we are unaware led him to emigrate to another climate, there seems to be no reason why he should not take some luggage, and even his interpreter, with him.

Mgr. Pelzer reminds us that, according to manuscript evidence, there were other translators of Aver-

roes besides Michael Scot: among them, master William
of Luna, at Naples, for the paraphrase of Porphyry's
*Isagoge*; and master Theodoric for the prologue to
the commentary on the *Physics*; in June, 1240, Herman the German translated Averroes's "middle commentary" on the *Nicomachean Ethics*, and in 1256
his "middle commentary" on the *Poetics*.

We may accept as a general conclusion that Averroes had not made his way into Paris before 1230.
The translation of his works probably extends over a
fairly considerable period; but one will admit, with
Fr. de Vaux, that the most important undertaking
took place at the court of Frederick II, round about
1230; not that Michael Scot could not have carried
on his work between 1220 and 1228, nor that other
translators could not have worked at the court of
Sicily before his arrival; but rather because translations of Averroes made either at Toledo before 1220,
or in Italy about the same date, would have been
known in Paris before 1230.

This general conclusion is confirmed by Roger
Bacon, for he also dates the entry of Aristotle into
the Christian world about this same year, 1230.

A magnificent manuscript in the Bibliothèque Na-
tionale in Paris, dated 1243, contains almost the complete *corpus* of the works of Averroes which were
known in the thirteenth century. This is valuable
evidence that the penetration of Averroes was virtually complete by about 1240.

The introduction of Averroes into the Christian
world was to have incalculable effects; his influence,
profound and often harmful, goes on until after the
Renaissance. But it will be some time before Latin
thinkers realize the true nature of Averroism, and

begin to be on their guard against its errors. Fr. Salman has shown that before 1250 scholastics received Averroes sympathetically, and with no sign of any misgiving. We shall come back to this point later.

The introduction of Averroes is the major event in the history of translation during the first half of the thirteenth century; but there are other undertakings of this kind which must at least be mentioned.

There are translations of Aristotle from Arabic into Latin: in this field we may mention Michael Scot's translation of the Arabian version of the *De Animalibus*, made at Toledo before 1220. The versions of Averroes are normally accompanied by the text of Aristotle which he is commenting on; thus we have next the *Metaphysics* translated from Arabic into Latin before 1240; it is in ten books (books II to X and book XII of our present editions), and is sometimes called *Metaphysica nova* in the manuscripts. We have also a whole series of new Latin translations of Aristotle from the Arabic; it may be noted that we have more exact information on some of them: Michael Scot is certainly the translator of the *De Caelo* and the *De Anima*; another translator from Toledo, Herman the German, translated the *Nicomachean Ethics* in 1240; an Alexandrine résumé of the same work in 1243 or 1244; the *Rhetoric* in 1250; and finally the *Poetics* in 1256.

Meanwhile, translations of Aristotle from Greek into Latin were also growing in number. Those which seem to be the earliest are anonymous; Mgr. Grabmann holds that the *Ethica Nova* was already in existence in 1210, and according to M. Franceschini the same is true of the *Metaphysica Media*. Various other fragments of the *Nicomachean Ethics* were circulating in the first half of the thirteenth century, and about 1240-1243, Robert Grosseteste in England began the first complete translation of the Greek *Nicomachean Ethics*; to him also we owe a version of the *De Caelo* up to the beginning of book III.

Among the scientific works of other writers, Greek, Arabian or Jewish, which were translated into Latin during the same period, the most important are the following: the *De Animalibus* of Avicenna, translated by Michael Scot at the court of Frederick II, about 1230; the *Guide for the Doubting* of Moses Maimonides, translated from Arabic into Hebrew, then from Hebrew into Latin in the first thirty years of the century; the works of Pseudo-Dionysius, the *De Orthodoxa Fide* of St. John Damascene, and some pseudo-Aristotelian opuscules—all done by Robert Grosseteste; and finally various works on medicine, mathematics and astronomy.

It will be noted that from the point of view of Aristotelianism, the period before 1250 is especially marked by the translation of the *Nicomachean Ethics*.

## The teaching of philosophy at Paris about 1240

Several historians have thought that when Gregory IX mitigated the measures taken against Aristotle in 1210 and 1215 it meant practically the abandonment of these measures. Hauréau saw in the letter of April 23rd, 1231, the abrogation of the decrees of 1210 and 1215; Mandonnet thought that the ban was maintained in principle but that in practice "little or no

notice was taken of it"; de Vaux also is inclined to
think that the penetration of Averroes, combined
with the attitude of Gregory IX, "modified the position into which Aristotle had been forced in the Parisian schools".

It seems to be an undeniable fact that there were
infringements of the decrees of 1210 and 1215 before
1231; we have the proof of that in the letter which
Gregory IX sent to the abbot of St. Victor and the
prior of St. James on April 20th, 1231; this letter
gave them power to absolve the masters and students
who had incurred excommunication by transgressing
the decrees of the Council of Paris and of Robert of
Courçon concerning the books of natural philosophy.
Since the threat of excommunication was not maintained in 1231, it seems probable that there were further transgressions after that date.

However, an important discovery enabled Mgr.
Grabmann to prove that the ban was on the whole
respected, at least for several years. This state of
affairs probably continued until about 1245; and the
official legislation of the Faculty of Arts, which was
modified only in 1252 and 1255, probably reflects
the usual teaching of the faculty.

In 1927 Mgr. Grabmann discovered in a Barcelona
manuscript (Ripoll 109) a most interesting anonymous document, which seems to have been written at
Paris between 1230 and 1240 by a master of the Faculty of Arts. This devoted professor realized the difficulties which faced candidates for academic degrees
—difficulties due to the diversity of subjects and the
variety of questions set by the examiners. He decided,
therefore, to compose a candidate's *vade-mecum*,
where the student would find set out, according to

the order in which the subjects appeared in the syllabus, the questions most often asked at examinations
and the replies which should be given. With this in
mind, he gives a methodical description of each of
the books used in the course, indicates its contents
and divisions, sets a certain number of questions relating to each section and provides a succinct reply.

The overwhelming interest of this document will
readily be perceived, especially after reading the various partial descriptions of it given by Mgr. Grabmann. It is to be hoped that some scholar will soon
give us the complete text of this most revealing document. Meanwhile, we will indicate here the points
given in the "examination-candidate's guide" touching
the history of Aristotelianism at Paris.

Our anonymous author begins his exposition with
some general considerations on philosophy; he sketches
its nature and structure, taking his lead from Boethius, as was the custom in works of logic in the
twelfth and particularly the thirteenth century;
briefly, he combines the old tripartite classification
(*rationalis, naturalis, moralis*) with the division into
*theoretical* and *practical* philosophy; further, he
adopts the division of theoretical philosophy according to the three degrees of abstraction; the *quadrivium* becomes a subdivision of the *Mathematica*, and
the *trivium* a subdivision of *Philosophia rationalis*.

As regards the text-books described by the author,
certain peculiarities must be pointed out.

—The *Liber de Causis* is given as the third part of
Aristotle's *Metaphysics*.

—Treating of astronomy, the author uses this obscure
phrase: "*Hec scientia traditur secundum unam sui partem in Tolomeo, secundum autem aliam partem tra-*

*ditur in Almagesto, et isti libri combusti sunt"*. Does he take Almagestus for an author ? Is the word *combusti* a copyist's error ? One can only conjecture.

—Alchemy is considered a subalternate science of meteorology, just as medicine is attached to psychology.

—The author does not know the origin of the *De Motu Cordis*, although he knows it is not Aristotle's: *"Hunc librum non fecit Aristoteles"*.

—Moral philosophy is divided from the point of view of the 'life of the soul', and the author is thus led to make theology or sacred science a practical science, a kind of supernatural ethics; this is a view which, as we have seen, corresponds fairly well to the tendencies of the Theology Faculty of Paris at the beginning of the century, and more generally, to the Augustinian conception of theological wisdom.

—For economic ethics, which the author calls *ypotica* (*"ab ypos, quod est sub, quod est scientia de subditis"*), Cicero is the only author considered; our document is not yet acquainted with the *Economics* or *Politics* of Aristotle.

—Plato's *Timaeus* and the *Consolation* of Boethius are attached to ethics, though in a rather indefinite manner: *"Ulterius notandum quod leguntur duo libri..."*

—In Grammar, Priscian is read, in conformity with the prescriptions of Robert of Courçon in 1215 and of Gregory IX in 1231.

—Finally, we may note that the document shows no knowledge of the author of the *Liber Sex Principiorum*.

But the most important observation that Mgr. Grabmann has made as a result of his study of the document is this. The subjects in this book, with its

clearly defined practical aim, receive very unequal
treatment. While the *Metaphysics* occupies scarcely
half a column, and the *Physics* little more than a
column in spite of its numerous *libri naturales*, more
than five columns are reserved for Aristotle's *Ethics*
alone (*Ethica Nova* and *Ethica Vetus*); that is to
say, 242 lines as against only 90 for the *Metaphysics*
and *Physics* combined. Further, the chapter on the
*Grammar* fills 23 columns, and the incomplete chapter on the *Logic* about 60. The difference of treatment is even more marked when we consider the
contents. For the *Physics* and *Metaphysics* the author
is content to indicate summarily the purpose of each
treatise and to add a few remarks of a general nature;
for the *Ethics*, *Grammar* and *Logic*, the *divisio textus*
is followed by a more or less considerable number of
questions concerning the work analysed and each
question receives a brief reply: thus the *De Interpretatione* has no less than 87 questions to its credit, the
*Priora Analytica* 63, the *Liber Elenchorum* 76, Porphyry's *Isagoge* 34. One very clear conclusion emerges
from these facts: at this period the *Metaphysics* and
the *Libri Naturales* of Aristotle were not expounded
in the Faculty of Arts at Paris. Their existence was
mentioned, perhaps a summary analysis of them was
given; but they were not used as text-books. This
fact, moreover, explains the total absence of Parisian
commentaries on these works before 1240.

There is one final fact that we must notice about
our "candidate's guide"; it is an interesting symptom of
the mentality which is growing up in the Faculty of
Arts in Paris, and which will shortly finish up as that
current of thought which we shall henceforth call
radical or heterodox Aristotelianism. The attitude we

are referring to shows itself in the questions raised in connexion with the *Ethics*; there, the philosophical conception of happiness is set in clear opposition to that of theology; the resurrection of the body is a miracle which does not correspond to natural laws, and with which philosophers have nothing to do [1].

Now this is quite correct, and one cannot but praise the anonymous author for separating so exactly the two fields. But at the same time, it is the starting point of those naturalistic and rationalist tendencies which will be condemned in 1277. Some scholars will soon be laying so much stress on the autonomy of the sciences that they will end up by putting philosophy and theology in an inadmissible juxtaposition; and the formulas which express this intellectual attitude will be taken by their adversaries as the expression of a double-truth.

For the moment, however, no such charge can be made against our anonymous author—quite the contrary; there is not a shadow of conflict between the two faculties, no suggestion of any uneasiness concerning the relations between reason and faith.

The anonymous collection of Barcelona is indeed a valuable guiding line for the historian who is trying to picture the growth of Aristotelianism as it appeared about the year 1240. On the other hand, with

---

[1] "*Item queritur utrum corpus sit natum recipere felicitatem sicut anima. Et videtur quod sic, cum sit instrumentum per quod anima operatur bonum, et ita videtur corpus mereri sicut anima. Ad hoc dicimus quod secundum theologos hoc habet veritatem, quia ponunt animam rejungi corpori post mortem. Sed hoc est plus per miraculum quam per naturam. Simpliciter enim hoc est innaturale, et ideo non ponitur a philosophis*".

the help of documents published by Mgr. Grabmann and some other scholars, it is possible to sketch in broad outline the history of the teaching of philosophy at Paris between 1230 and 1250. It will be seen that the details furnished by this literature fit perfectly with those given by the Barcelona document.


## The Philosophical Literature


Up to about 1240, the literary production of the philosophers of Paris deals almost exclusively with logic. It shows that these masters had a profound knowledge of the treatises of the *Organon* and the commentaries on it, as well as a remarkable skill in the use of Aristotelian logic.

The earliest of these professors of logic at Paris who is actually known to us is John Pagus. He is quoted in a letter from Gregory IX to St. Louis, dated May 6th, 1231; the Pope recommends to the king's favour masters Godfrey of Poitiers and William of Auxerre, who are returning from Rome where they have been dealing with the Pope concerning university affairs during the academic strike of 1229-1231. Later on, the Pope's letter links master John Pagus (*Johannem Pagium*) with the other two, and puts the king on his guard against any suspicion he may have conceived about them. At that time, John Pagus must have been a master in the Faculty of Arts, as he appears as a mere bachelor of theology about 1240-1242; perhaps he was the representative of the Faculty of Arts in the university delegation which went to Rome at Gregory IX's request; or perhaps he accompanied

William of Auxerre in his journey to Rome at the beginning of 1230. The court was in conflict with the university in the matter which had brought about the suspension of lectures, and it is therefore quite understandable that the delegates on their return from Rome should have provided themselves with a letter of recommendation from the Pope, assuring the king that they have done nothing detrimental to his honour or interest. The philosophical career of John Pagus, therefore, covers a period about 1230, and he must have begun his theological studies about 1231-1235, since he was a bachelor of theology about 1240-1242. We have three of his works on logic: the *Apellationes*, the *Syncategoremata*, and the *Rationes super Predicamenta Aristotelis*.

There is good reason to think that the English logician, William of Shyreswood, taught at Paris, and that he was the master of Peter of Spain there. Since Peter himself taught at Paris before leaving for Sienna, where he is found in 1246, his studies must no doubt have taken place well before this, probably before 1240. Master William, then, must have been teaching at Paris at more or less the same time as William of St. Amour, who will be dealt with shortly. Roger Bacon, who holds his fellow-countryman in high esteem (*longe sapientior Alberto, nam in philosophia communi nullus major est eo*), could have known him in Paris. Between 1255 and 1257, William became treasurer of Lincoln cathedral, and he was still occupying that post in 1267, when Roger Bacon was writing his *Opus Tertium*. He died between 1267 and 1279. His principal work, the *Summulae Logicales*, is known from a single manuscript, kept in Paris; in this manuscript the work also bears the title: *Intro-*

*ductiones Magistri Gulielmi de Shyreswood in logi-
cam*. Mgr. Grabmann has published the complete text.
This little manual of formal logic contains six chapters: *De propositione, De predicabili, De syllogismo,
De locis dialecticis, De proprietatibus terminorum, De
fallaciis*. William is also the author of another work
on logic, this time preserved in two manuscripts: the
*Syncategoremata*, of which Mgr. Grabmann has published the introduction. Like the previous work, this
treatise was written at Paris, for this city is quoted
by the author in the examples he uses to illustrate the
rules of logic. Finally, there are three other opuscules
on logic which should probably be restored to William. They are found in the Paris manuscript after
the *Summulae Logicales* and the *Syncategoremata*, and
are called: *Insolubilia* (on apparently insoluble sophisms), *Obligationes* (on the function of the *respondens*
and *opponens* in academic debates), and the *Petitio-
nes Contrariorum* (on sophisms which rest on contradictory presuppositions).

Peter of Spain, disciple of William of Shyreswood, is
more famous than his master. He was born in Lisbon,
was master in Paris till about 1246 and professor at
Sienna in 1246. Archbishop of Braga in 1272, cardinal in 1273, he became Pope under the name of
John XXI in September, 1276, and died in May, 1277.
It was he who initiated the enquiry which resulted
in the great condemnation of Aristotelianism on
March 7th, 1277. Like his master, William, he is the
author of a manual of logic, the *Summulae Logicales*.
But this treatise had a much greater success than its
predecessor, and was for many centuries the classical
manual for the teaching of logic. It is thus found
in innumerable manuscripts, was frequently com-

mented on, and has been reprinted several times from 1480 onwards. Peter is also the author of two other works on logic identified by Mgr. Grabmann: the *Tractatus Majorum Fallaciorum* and the *Syncategoremata*. While these works on logic probably belong to Peter's Parisian period, one may conjecture that his works on natural philosophy belong rather to his Italian period, after 1245. Mgr. Grabmann, again, discovered the important *Liber de Anima*, a real *summa* of psychology, the earliest systematic exposition of Aristotle's psychology. The work contains thirteen treatises, subdivided into chapters. The *explicit* runs as follows: *"Ego igitur Petrus Hispanus Portugalensis liberalium artium doctor, philosophice sublimitatis gubernator, medicinalis facultatis decor ac proficue rector, in scientia anime decrevi hoc opus precipuum componendum, pro cujus complemento divine bonitatis largitas gratiarum actionibus exaltetur"*. At that time, therefore, the author was rector of the faculty of medicine, but he does not say in what university. He uses Aristotle and the Arabians, though without quoting them; and he puts his medical knowledge to good use in his exposition of the vital functions. Finally, Mgr. Grabmann has restored several commentaries on Aristotle to Peter: on the *De Animalibus*, on the *De Morte et Vita*, on the *De Anima*; and a commentary on the writings of Pseudo-Dionysius.

Mgr. Grabmann has also found commentaries on the two *Analytics* composed by William of St. Amour, the celebrated adversary of the Mendicant Friars, while he was teaching in the Arts Faculty, from 1236 to 1247.

Lambert of Auxerre taught logic in Paris around 1250. His *Summulae Logicales* are still unpublished,

apart from fragments edited by Hauréau and Prantl.
M. Michalski thought that Peter of Spain depended on
Lambert, but Mgr. Grabmann inclined to the opposite
view, that Lambert used the manual of Peter of Spain.

The most prolific of the professors of logic at Paris
towards the middle of the thirteenth century was
Nicholas of Paris. We possess three of his commentaries
on the *Isagoge* of Porphyry, commentaries on the *Categories*, the *De Interpretatione*, the *Posterior Analytics*, the *Liber Sex Principiorum* attributed to Gilbert
of la Porrée, the *De Differentiis Topicis* and the *De
Divisione* of Boethius, not to mention his logico-
grammatical glosses on the writings of Donatus and
Priscian. Besides formal logic, Nicholas was also interested in speculative grammar and the problem of
the classification of the sciences. He was still teaching
in 1263.

When the literary production of these masters has
been studied carefully and given its exact place in the
history of logic, it will be possible to date other
works, anonymous and unpublished, by relation to
them.

For the masters of the Middle Ages, logic was not
only a speculative science; it was also, perhaps more
so, an art. One had to know how to use skilfully this
universal instrument of knowledge; the *magister artium* had to know all the secrets of debate and of
scientific demonstration. Thus, at a very early date
we find practical exercises taking their place in the
course side by side with lectures on theory. These
academic jousts gave rise to a special type of literature,
examples of which are found in many scholastic manuscripts. Mgr. Grabmann called it *die Sophismata-
literatur*; and in the monograph which he devoted to

the subject, he showed that these exercises in sophistry were already in existence in the twelfth century; he described a whole series of unpublished documents relating to these exercises, belonging to the twelfth, thirteenth and fourteenth centuries. It is probable that many of these documents emanate from scholastic circles in Paris in the first half of the thirteenth century.

The works on logic take up nearly all the literary activity of the philosophers of Paris before the middle of the thirteenth century; but alongside them we find some commentaries on the *Ethics,* the teaching of which, it will be remembered, had been permitted by Robert of Courçon. The discovery of these works is the fruit of Dom Lottin's researches. He has brought to light three commentaries on the *Nicomachean Ethics* which are prior to the complete translation of this work by Robert Grosseteste about 1240-1243. The first two (A and P) are confined to the *Ethica Vetus* (books two and three of the *Nicomachean Ethics*), and both are incomplete, at least in the only copy of them so far found. The third (F) contains the *Ethica Nova* (book one of the *Nicomachean Ethics*) and the *Ethica Vetus.* The first is no doubt very early, since it seems to be unacquainted with the *Ethica Nova.* The second quotes Averroes and must therefore be dated between 1230 and 1240. The third is probably contemporary with the preceding.

As for the method adopted in these commentaries, each lecture contains first of all the *expositio litterae,* then a certain number of *quaestiones* suggested by Aristotle's text, dealing with psychological and moral problems.

Dom Lottin has carried out a most revealing enquiry into these unpublished texts in order to find out their attitude to a series of questions which were classical in the thirteenth century: the distinction between the soul and its faculties, the plurality of souls in man, active and possible intellect, free will, infused and acquired virtue, intellectual and moral virtue, moral good and evil. Dom Lottin has published extensive fragments of these three commentaries. We cannot do better than reproduce the results of his enquiry, adding a few personal reflexions.

These writings on morality reveal an undeniable relationship between the teaching in the Faculty of Arts and that of the Theological Faculty; we find clear references to the theological problems which were discussed at the time. For the first (A) and the third (F), Dom Lottin is inclined to admit some dependence on Philip the Chancellor. The second (P) betrays the influence of theology and of Aristotle, but also, although in a moderate degree, that of Avicenna, in his manner of conceiving the two intellects, active and possible.

As for the mentality displayed by these documents, Dom Lottin writes apropos of the passages distinguishing between infused and acquired virtue: "These texts are worth quoting. They show clearly that far from contradicting the teaching of the Faculty of Theology, these masters of arts integrated it into their lectures, while underlining the philosophical viewpoint which was theirs. One would seek in vain in these texts for any passage which proclaims, even remotely, the famous theory of double truth". And at the conclusion of his study, the author expresses himself as follows: "At the time we are dealing with, conflict has not yet broken out between a theology made up of the Augustinian tradition and an innovating philosophy claiming the authority of Aristotle. The scholars of the Arts Faculty quote St. Augustine often. They are careful to abandon Avicenna's theory of the active intellect, which is scarcely reconcilable with dogma. They find no difficulty in accepting the views of the theologians on the infused virtues, the only true virtues. Our masters of arts want nothing better than to live in perfect understanding with their powerful neighbours, the accredited guardians of orthodoxy".

It will be seen that we have here exactly the same attitude as that which we met in the "examination-candidate's guide" analysed above. In both, there is the same clear recognition of the differences of *method* and *doctrine* which exist between theology and philosophy. And while Dom Lottin is perfectly right in saying that the atmosphere of conflict is absent, nevertheless it must be recognised that there are difficulties present under the surface; and it only needs some master of arts to press too strongly the philosophical viewpoint on some matter where it is incompatible with that of theology, for these difficulties to break to the surface. Here is a significant detail: we find here, ready made, the expressions which Siger of Brabant will use later on: *"loquendo secundum philosophos; sed quia hic non debemus solvere quemadmodum theologi, sed secundum intentionem philosophi, ideo dicendum est aliter; loquendo secundum theologos et secundum veritatem"*. Notice the last phrase, where the theological point of view is identified with that of truth, as later in the writings of Siger. Another significant detail is the fact that our moralists seem to take an almost coquettish delight in referring to God in the manner of the pagan philosophers: *"primum, prima intelligentia"* [1].

As far as can be judged, the texts published by Dom Lottin seem to have some doctrinal analogies with the anonymous Barcelona document described above, as well as with the *Liber de Anima* of Peter of Spain.

In connexion with the teaching of the *Ethics* before 1250, we must mention a *Compendium* of the *Ethica Nova et Vetus* preserved in a manuscript at Munich; and a *Tabula*, that is to say, an alphabetical lexicon of terms taken from the *Ethica Nova* and the *Ethica Vetus*; this document was found by Mgr. Grabmann in a manuscript at Pisa.

Thus, up to about 1240, all the literary production of the Faculty of Arts in Paris was, as far as our present information goes, connected with logic, ethics or grammar. This is in striking contrast with what is going on at Oxford. There, we find that Aristotle's *Libri Naturales* and *Metaphysics* have been commented on by the masters since the beginning of the century. It is certain, then, that the effects of the interdicts of 1210 and 1215, continued in 1231 by Gregory IX, were felt in Paris until at least about 1240.

---

[1] The author of the second of the three commentaries (P), puts forward this piquant comparison: *"Intellectus enim agens se habet ad intellectum possibilem sicut monachus claustralis ad abbatem: monachus enim debet habere vitam contemplativam, sed abbas debet habere vitam contemplativam et activam: unde multi sunt boni monachi qui non essent boni abbates".*

Roger Bacon is the first, as far as is actually known, to bear witness to a modification of this state of things [1]. We can fix the period when Bacon was teaching in Paris at about 1245. His commentaries on Aristotle and Proclus (*Liber de Causis*), preserved in the famous manuscript 406 of Amiens library, are transcripts of notes taken during these lectures, and are thus the earliest evidence of the teaching of the *Physics* and *Metaphysics* in the Arts Faculty of Paris. We are faced with an impressive *corpus* of commentaries; two on the *Physics*, four on the *Metaphysics*, commentaries on the pseudo-Aristotelian works *De Plantis* and *De Causis*, not to mention several commentaries on other works of Aristotle which are no longer to be found.

One question occurs to us immediately: how was it possible for Bacon to teach the *Libri Naturales* at Paris when they fell under the ban issued in 1210, renewed in 1215 and 1231, and faithfully observed till at least about 1240 ? Such an innovation could not have passed unnoticed. How is that it did not raise any protest ? We can hardly suggest an intervention on the part of Rome, modifying the legal position of Aristotle at Paris; in the first place, it would be impossible to explain why such an intervention has left no trace in contemporary documents; and, in the second place, we know that on September 22nd, 1245, Innocent IV sent a letter to the university of Toulouse, applying to this university the statutes

[1] Thirty years later, Bacon implicitly states that he was one of the first to comment on natural philosophy at Paris. In 1267, he writes: "*Naturalis philosophia Aristotelis quae vix a triginta annis lecta est, et a paucis viris, et a quibus scripta non sunt facta, adhuc sciri non poterit apud vulgum*".

which Gregory IX had promulgated for the university
of Paris; thus, far from being withdrawn, the ban
on the reading of the *Libri Naturales* was extended to
Toulouse, which had hitherto boasted of its escape.
We are inclined to think that the prohibition which
was upheld in 1231 became a dead letter at Paris
after the death of Gregory IX (August 22nd, 1241),
and that the *Libri Naturales* began to be read during
the troubled period which the Roman church passed
through between the death of Gregory and the elec-
tion of Innocent IV (June 25th, 1243). This important
innovation was able to be made without resistance
because the atmosphere at Paris was at that moment
entirely favourable to Aristotle. Roger Bacon came
from Oxford, where the complete works of Aristotle
had long been commented on; he could point out to
his colleagues that the Faculty of Arts in Paris was in
a state of intolerable inferiority in relation to its
English rival; that the situation created by the Council of Paris was unreasonable and unjust; and finally,
that there was no serious foundation for this continued mistrust of Aristotle. The Faculty of Arts was
receptive to such suggestions. And no doubt their
attitude was not very different from that which pre-
vailed in theological circles, and even in the episcopal
curia; the Bishop of Paris, William of Auvergne, made
abundant use of Aristotle and even, as we have seen,
received favourably the commentaries of Averroes.
We shall have to point out in a moment to what an
extent the majority of theologians at this time were
already won over to the cause of Aristotelianism, and
how warmly they at first welcomed his Arabian commentator. Why then should the theologians who made
such free use of the treatises of Aristotle prevent

their philosophical colleagues from reading and commenting on him ?

Once he had gained a footing, Aristotle had come to stay; and the Church never again thought seriously about banishing him. Certainly, Urban IV on January 19th, 1263, confirmed Gregory IX's statutes of 1231, and the passage relating to the *Libri Naturales* was not suppressed; but we shall see later that the influence of this act does not seem to have been very considerable. In 1277, in the great condemnation of peripatetic philosophy, no one thinks of repeating or recalling the interdicts of earlier days. And a century later, in 1366, Urban V's legates make the knowledge of the complete works of Aristotle compulsory for candidates to the licentiate in arts [1].

To return to Roger Bacon: whether it was Bacon himself or others before him who began lecturing on Aristotle's *Physics* and *Metaphysics*, this move seems to have been welcomed as a happy step forward, marking the end of an impossible situation which no longer corresponded to the scientific needs of the times. The step appeared so natural that it raised no opposition on the part of the religious or academic authorities.

Bacon's commentaries are neither paraphrases in the manner of Avicenna or Albert the Great, nor literal commentaries like those of Averroes or St. Thomas Aquinas. They are series of questions suggested by

[1] The Church could not in fact simply condemn Aristotle, and did not want to. But neither could she welcome him without reserve, constituting as he undoubtedly did a danger to Christian thought. This explains the attitude of prudence and caution, which later events showed to be so opportune, and which ceased as soon as Aristotelianism was sufficiently assimilated. There was, then, no inconsistency in the Church's conduct in this matter.

Aristotle's text, and treated according to the classical method of the *sic et non*, exactly as Siger of Brabant does later.

Mgr. Grabmann has made a special analysis of the *Quaestiones Alterae supra Libros Physicorum*, and has been struck by the relative maturity of this commentary, and by the very personal ideas it expresses. Fr. Delorme draws attention to the historical importance of the *Quaestiones*, and points out some of its characteristics: it proves to us, he says, that a whole world of philosophical ideas was under discussion in the Faculty of Arts; it shows us how well Bacon had assimilated Aristotle's *Physics* and *Metaphysics*; after Aristotle, the authors most often used are Avicenna, Averroes and Boethius, though Bacon is sometimes rather harsh in his treatment of Averroes, especially concerning the eternity of the world: Bacon held that Aristotle did not positively teach the eternity of the world, and that it was Averroes who was responsible for this pejorative interpretation of Aristotle's text. On the other hand, Fr. Salman has shown that the young Bacon, while he was master in Paris, did not see the most characteristic doctrine of Averroes in psychology, namely monopsychism : according to Bacon, Averroes thought that the active and possible intellects were two powers of the individual soul !

Fr. Crowley's conclusions are particularly interesting. The examination of Bacon's hylomorphic doctrine shows that he holds several theses which are generally attributed to the old traditional school, called "Augustinian". So, for example, he teaches universal hylomorphism; and is familiar with nearly all the arguments used by subsequent defenders of this theory; his hylomorphism is an amalgam of ideas taken from

Aristotle, Avicebron, Averroes and Gundissalinus; he never appeals to the authority of St.Augustine for this doctrine. The whole of Bacon's psychology is penetrated with non-Aristotelian elements, and again the influence of St. Augustine is negligible; the basis is Aristotelian, but there is considerable Arabian influence, especially in the doctrine of the two intellects (Avicenna, Algazel, Averroes); and there is the same syncretism in the theory of knowledge. A more general conclusion emerges from Fr. Crowley's enquiry: "The term *Augustinianism* cannot be used to describe the philosophical teaching of the period prior to St.Thomas. The influence of St.Augustine on Bacon is practically absent. If we leave aside Christian influences, the most adequate description of Bacon's philosophy would be to call it a *neo-Platonic Aristotelianism*" [1].

It may be added that this philosophy does not yet bear the marks of a solid synthesis; like all the philosophers of this period, Bacon is feeling his way; Latin Aristotelianism has not yet emerged from the eclectic stage which is characteristic of any system in its formative period. This is what gives such considerable historical interest to Bacon's *Quaestiones*: they reflect the teaching of the Faculty of Arts of Paris at the moment when Aristotelianism was taking definite root there.

Many other names should find their place in the portrait-gallery of masters who taught philosophy at Pa-

---

[1] See *Revue Néoscolastique d. Philosophie*, November 1939, pp. 648-650, and especially TH. CROWLEY, *Roger Bacon. The Problem of the Soul in his Philosophical Commentaries*, Louvain-Dublin, 1950.

ris in the first half of the thirteenth century. Some
are still completely unknown. Others have already
been brought to the attention of scholars: Robert Kilwardby, for example, who taught in the Faculty of
Arts in Paris before 1250; if the philosophical works
attributed to him by the catalogue of Stams are
really his, he would merit attentive study; and in any
case he has composed, probably about 1250, the most
remarkable introduction to philosophy which the
Middle Ages have produced, the *De Ortu et Divisione
Philosophiae*.

## The Theological Literature

To complete our enquiry into Aristotelianism in Paris between 1230 and 1250, we must now go over
to the camp of the theologians and ask them about
their attitude to Aristotle. It is an immense task, for,
as Mgr. Pelzer observes: "The use which was made
of Aristotle when he was first introduced is a subject
which is only now, following Baeumker, beginning to
be studied seriously.". We will limit ourselves here to
fairly general conclusions, drawing on the research
published to date.

We know already that, at the end of the twelfth
and the beginning of the thirteenth century, the theological school at Paris was rather opposed to the use of
dialectic in the elaboration of the sacred science. We
have mentioned in what sense one can speak of Augustinianism in connection with this school. Following Mgr. Grabmann, we have shown that the Faculty
of Theology was probably not a mere bystander in
the events of 1210 and 1215. Now between 1210 and
1230 two divergent trends begin to appear in the fa-

culty. Some remain faithful to the traditional orientation of ideas, and protest against the inroads which
philosophy is making into the sacred science; we hear
the echo of these complaints in Gregory IX's letters of
1228 and 1231. Others are influenced by the new
philosophical literature, and allow philosophical speculation more and more scope in theology. After
1230, the new trend rapidly gets the upper hand,
and it is the growth of this new school which must
now occupy our attention.

Even before 1200, the influence of the recently
discovered Aristotle could be seen in the *Disputatio-
nes* of the Parisian master Simon of Tournai: he seems
to have been acquainted with the *Physics, Metaphysics* and the *De Anima,* and for him the expressions
*doctrina aristotelica* and *philosophia* are synonymous.
But the real pioneers of the new method were Philip
the Chancellor, William of Auxerre and William of
Auvergne, all three of whom were teaching about
1225.

William of Auxerre's *Summa Aurea* shows only a
slight influence of the new philosophy; but in Philip's
*Summa de Bono,* published ten years later, there are
indications of a much wider literary context. Philip
quotes Aristotle (especially the *Ethics*) and Averroes,
but he is subject to many other influences also; in his
treatise on the transcendental properties—the first of
its kind—he depends on St. Augustine and St. Anselm, Pseudo-Dionysius and Boethius, Aristotelianism
and neo-Platonism. "These last two", as Dom Pouillon
concludes, "merge into one, with perhaps a slight
predominance of neo-Platonism".

"The line of great speculative theologians opens
with William of Auvergne, one of the most original

minds of the first half of the century... William
is the first great philosopher of the thirteenth century": so writes M. De Wulf. Without neglecting the
Latin and Augustinian tradition, he makes copious,
though judicious, use of Aristotle: *"Quamquam autem in multis contradicendum sit Aristoteli, sicut
revera dignum et justum est, et hoc in omnibus ser-
monibus quibus contradicit veritati, sic suscipiendus
est, id est sustinendus, in eis omnibus in quibus recte
sensisse invenitur"*. He knows and uses many other
philosophers, Greek, Jewish and Arab, and with all
of them displays the same independence of judgment. He opposes vigorously the materialism of
Alexander of Aphrodisias; he combats the heresies of
the Catharists, Albigensians and Amalricians; he
condemns several Arabian doctrines, including some
of the errors of Avicenna; he extends his approval
to Averroes and Maimonides, and especially to the
Jew Avicebron, whom he takes to be a Christian
and proclaims *"unicus omnium philosophantium no-
bilissimus"*.

In Renan's opinion, William of Auvergne was the
first Latin adversary of Averroistic monopsychism,
although William does not explicitly attribute the
paternity of this error to Averroes. But Fr. de Vaux
has since established that, in the texts referred to by
Renan, William was opposing Avicennianism, not
Averroism. And there is no foundation at all for the
view that William had in mind Parisian masters holding Averroistic doctrines.

After William of Auvergne, the doctrinal influence
of the secular masters undergoes an eclipse until the
time of Godfrey of Fontaines and Henry of Ghent.
By intensive recruiting in university circles, the men-

dicant orders attracted the elite of the academic po-
pulation, and took serious toll of the ranks of the
seculars; and on the other hand, the seculars wasted
the best part of their energies in sterile opposition to
the mendicants and in other quarrels.

How should one describe the *philosophical* position
of the masters just mentioned ? It is very difficult
to give it a definite label, so disparate are the various
sources drawn on in these first essays in theological
speculation. In any case, it is clear that the label
"Augustinianism" does not fit the facts, any more
than that of "Aristotelianism". Aristotelian influence,
however, does predominate; the thought of these first
speculative theologians had been formed and fixed by
Aristotelian dialectic; along with this logic, many
fundamental metaphysical notions penetrated their
minds, and others came to them from Jewish or Arabian sources, especially from Avicenna, and then from
Averroes and Maimonides. On the philosophical plane,
therefore, we have an *eclectic Aristotelianism*, or a
*"neo-Platonizing" Aristotelianism*, in various stages
of development; the shades of difference and the
internal structure of each must be determined in every
particular case. And finally, we must not forget that
we are dealing with theological works; all this
philosophical speculation takes place in a theological
framework, and consequently in an Augustinian
spirit.

Alexander of Hales was English by birth. He studied
arts and theology in Paris about 1215-1225 and was
professor of sacred science presumably from 1226;
but he entered the Friars Minor about 1236 and so
became the first holder of the Franciscan chair of

theology, which he occupied till 1238 or 1241. John of la Rochelle succeeded him and they both died in 1245. It is not for us to explain how the Franciscans of Paris and Oxford passed, in less than ten years, from the primitive ideal of St. Francis to the very different conception implied by the scientific and professorial activity they display after 1230. All we need to notice is the fact that the work of the first two Franciscan *"regentes"* shows the influence of pagan philosophy, quite as much as that of their contemporaries Philip the Chancellor and William of Auvergne.

The *Summa Universae Theologiae* attributed to Alexander is actually a fairly late compilation, finished only after 1256. John of la Rochelle is its real promoter, and considerable parts of the book are from his pen. John was very receptive to philosophical ideas. M. De Wulf writes of him: "He used almost all Aristotle's philosophical works. Aristotle's stock was beginning to rise about 1231, and John contributed not a little to his decisive success; but that does not prevent John from criticizing him, and departing from him on important questions. He also made use of the Arabian commentators, especially Avicenna, sometimes praising him, sometimes criticizing. At the same time, he gives pride of place to a number of Platonic and Augustinian doctrines from twelfth century scholasticism, so much so that he can write: *Plus credendum est Augustino et Anselmo quam Aristoteli.* In the evolution of ideas, then, his attitude is typical, and he is a significant representative of the movement which is commonly called Augustinian". M. De Wulf has, more than anyone else, stressed the fact that this last epithet calls for great reservations when it is applied to thinkers like Alexander who add a whole series of new philosophical conceptions from Aristotle, Avicenna and others to the Augustinian traditions of Latin theology.

John of la Rochelle's *Summa de Anima* betrays similar influences, as well as the syncretism which is common to all the masters of this period. According to Fr. Minges, his theory of knowledge puts side by side the doctrines of Aristotle, Augustine, Avicenna and John Damascene, without being able to reconcile them.

John's successor, Eudes Rigaud, who taught from 1245 to 1248, shows a certain mistrust of the *philosophantes*, who are too servile in following Aristotle.

There can be no question of subscribing to the paeans which Fr. Jules d'Albi addresses to the first Franciscan masters, especially Alexander of Hales. No doubt their merits are considerable, and the great scholastics who come after them owe more to them than is generally thought. But we must see them in their proper light, as initiators; we must not pretend that in 1245 "the scholastic movement was in full swing"; nor should we attribute to them the merit of having begun "the movement to assimilate peripatetic philosophy" at Paris. Well before their time, the religious authorities had had to moderate the zeal of the Arts Faculty for Aristotle; and the speculative trend in theology had received great encouragement from bishop and chancellor before the Franciscan chair was set up. On the other hand, Fr. d'Albi is right when he says that the first Franciscans welcomed Aristotle more warmly and with less hesitation than the first Dominicans, at least in Paris.

It will remembered that the Dominicans were forbidden by their Constitutions of 1228 to study profane sciences or liberal arts unless they had a dispensation. The first masters at Paris kept to that
rule, which was after all, as Fr. Mandonnet observes,
the rule adopted by the Roman church since the
middle of the twelfth century, and was in conformity
with the very firm directives of Gregory IX in his
letter of July 7th, 1228.

The first Dominican *magister regens,* Roland of
Cremona, had been a brilliant professor of philosophy
(perhaps of medicine also) at Bologna before entering
the order in 1219. Thus he is in full sympathy with
the new philosophical literature, and his *Summa Theologica,* sometimes wrongly called *Quaestiones super
Quatuor Libros Sententiarum,* shows an extensive
knowledge of Aristotle. It was composed after his
stay in Paris, about 1234. His Parisian period was
only transitory, from 1228 to 1230, and his immediate successors in one or other of the Dominican
chairs were much more conservative. John of St.
Giles, Hugh of St. Cher, Guerric of St. Quentin, all
remained aloof from the philosophical movement. As
for the doctrinal tendencies of the first Dominican
masters, we cannot better describe them than by
adopting the conclusions reached by Fr. J. Martin,
O.P., as a result of a study he made some thirty
years ago: "Unity of thought and consistency of doctrine are too often lacking in these first Dominican
masters for us to be able to say that they formed a
school in the proper sense of the term. Each wrote
under the influence of his own environment, they
followed different routes, and tried to establish their
own individual, sometimes peculiar, conclusions. It is

impossible to form a theological system from their doctrines. By the same fact, it becomes impossible to maintain the existence of an Augustinian school among the early Dominicans. All we can do is to examine how far these doctors adhered, each in his own way, to theories which were described at the time as the doctrines of St. Augustine". The author adds that the exposition of theological Augustinianism as it is found in the article by Fr. Portalié in the *Dictionnaire de Théologie Catholique* does not, on the whole, apply to any of the Dominican authors he has studied. Need we add that there can be still less question of the *philosophical* Augustinianism of these masters ?

The sojourn of Albert the Great at Paris marks a decisive turning point in the history of Dominican studies and in the history of Aristotelianism. This period coincides almost exactly with the last years of William of Auvergne's life (he died in 1249) ; with the period when John of la Rochelle was *"regens"* in the Franciscan order (1238-1245) ; with the period when Peter of Spain (before 1246), William of St. Amour (1236-1247), and Roger Bacon (about 1240-1247) were teaching philosophy, as also perhaps Lambert of Auxerre and Nicholas of Paris. These years of Albert the Great's life, then, fit perfectly into the framework of our enquiry into Aristotelianism at Paris before 1250.

The chronology of Albert the Great's life and especially of his works is by no means completely established, although historical research on the subject took a great step forward through the numerous works published on the occasion of his canonization by pope Pius XI in 1931. Albert of Lauingen was born in 1206 or at the beginning of 1207 (perhaps in 1200

or even earlier as used to be held before the publications of Fr. Mandonnet and as some scholars still accept
today). He made his first university studies at Bologna and Padua; but it should be noted that his stay
in the Italian schools was of short duration—he arrived in Bologna in 1222, went to Padua the same
year, took the Dominican habit in the August of
1223, and was immediately sent to their house in
Cologne to pursue his studies. From these facts one
may conclude that Roger Bacon is speaking the truth
when he says that Albert never learnt philosophy in
the schools and never taught it. From 1228 to 1240,
Albert lectured in theology in various houses throughout Germany. In 1240, he arrived in Paris to gain his
theological degrees; he lectured on the *Sentences* as
bachelor from 1240 to 1242, and from 1242 to 1248
occupied one of the two Dominican chairs as *magister
regens*. He then returned to Cologne to found there
the Dominican *Studium generale*; became provincial
over the province of Germany (1254-1257), resumed
his teaching in Cologne (1257-1260), and then occupied the episcopal see of Ratisbon (1260-1262).
The last eighteen years of his life, from 1262 to
1280, were spent in intense activity in many directions—preaching, travelling, diplomatic missions,
scientific research, publications of all kinds.

When Albert arrived at Paris in 1240, at the age
of thirty-four (according to Mandonnet), he found
a university world which was seething with activity.
William of Auvergne was Bishop of Paris; John of la
Rochelle had just succeeded his old master, Alexander
of Hales, in the Franciscan chair of theology; in the
Faculty of Arts, masters of note were teaching Aristotle's logic, ethics, and perhaps his physics and meta-

physics also. Two of Albert's great theological works belong to this period of his life: the *Summa de Creaturis* and the commentary *In Libros Sententiarum*. Both of them bear witness to an assiduous study of philosophical works. Concerning the *Summa de Creaturis*, Fr. de Vaux writes: "The abundance of information found in this work, as compared with the relative poverty of a previous book, the *Tractatus de Natura Boni*, written while he was in Germany, gives us some idea of the literature which Albert found on arriving at the Parisian *Studium*". However, his contact with philosophy dates from long before his arrival in Paris: the treatise just mentioned, *De Natura Boni*, is his first theological work, written about 1236 or 1237, and is rather a work on practical ethics; even in this, his quotations are taken by preference from the philosophers. Dom Lottin writes: "Cicero appears about twenty times, as often even as St. Augustine. But beyond all doubt, Aristotle is his favourite—he is mentioned nearly forty times. In isolated quotations, he refers to the *De Reminiscentia*, the *De Anima*, the *De Caelo et Mundo*, the *Metaphysics* and the *Physics*; the other quotations are from the *Ethics*" [1]. It is clear that Albert took advantage of the dispensation provided for in the Constitutions of 1228. This is quite understandable; since he had hardly begun his studies in the liberal arts when he

[1] Dom Lottin concludes his enquiry in these terms: "Albert must have acquired the immense erudition which he displays from the very first page of the *Summa de Creaturis* some time between the years 1236-1237, the date of the *De Natura Boni*, and 1240-1241, when the *Summa de Creaturis* was written". *Recherches de Théologie Ancienne et Médiévale*, 1932, p. 82. But it is probable, as Fr. de Vaux suggests, that Albert found new sources at Paris, including the works of Averroes.

entered religion, he had to continue them as a member of the order.

So Albert made abundant use of philosophical works in the first theological books he wrote at Paris. There is no doubt that he marks a new step forward in this direction as compared with William of Auvergne and Alexander of Hales; but the progress is quantitative rather than qualitative; Aristotelian influence is more extensive in Albert, but he does not arrive at a synthesis greatly superior to that of his contemporaries. Both treat of the same problems, both move in the same realm of ideas and doctrines. We are still dealing with first attempts at theological systematisation, in which traditional elements come face to face with the new philosophy.

It is still disputed whether it was in Paris that Albert began the great work of his life, the *corpus* of Aristotelian paraphrases. Fr. Mandonnet was of the opinion that the date of composition of the bulk of Albert's philosophical work could be fixed between 1245 and 1256. Fr. Pelster, on the other hand, puts them between 1248 and 1275 and thinks that the majority of them were composed between 1256 and 1270. Many critics have accepted Fr. Mandonnet's conclusions, but nowadays most follow Fr. Pelster's, while some are still doubtful.

Whichever opinion we follow, it is certain that Albert's Aristotelian *corpus* could not have been more than begun at Paris. All the paraphrases which can be dated are later than 1248; and moreover, the years when he was teaching in Paris must have been largely taken up with his theological works; at the beginning there was the explanation of the *Sentences* and the composition of the *Summa de Creaturis*, later his duties as *"regens"* (teaching and direction of academic debates), and finally, the redaction of the *Commentary on the Sentences.*

It is hardly likely, then, that Albert began his paraphrases at Paris. When he came back to Cologne in 1248, he began commenting on the writings of Pseudo-Dionysius and the *Nicomachean Ethics*; his interests, then, were still the same as before; he was still dealing with theology and ethics. If he had begun his great encyclopaedia of natural philosophy at Paris, it would be hard to understand why he should break off and take up work of such a very different kind.

And in any case, the circulation and influence of the Aristotelian commentaries certainly puts them outside the scope of the period we have dealt with up till now, that is to say, the first half of the thirteenth century. Therefore, since our plan is to retrace the progress of Latin Aristotelianism in its true historical perspective, we will reserve this work for a later stage of the enquiry.

This rapid sketch of the theological movement between 1230 and 1250 enables us to draw a general conclusion concerning the penetration of Aristotelianism in the Theological Faculty. While the reading of the *Libri Naturales* was still forbidden to the Faculty of Arts, the majority of theologians, or at least the most famous of them, were consulting and using the writings of Aristotle and the other pagan philosophers which they had at their disposition. Little by little, an atmosphere was created which was favourable to the study of pagan philosophy and its use in theology. This did not take place without some resistance, which was particularly acute among the Dominicans, as appears from the bitter complaints of Albert the Great. However, the philosophy used by the theologians was lacking in cohesion; it was an Aristotelianism which was not yet fully assimilated, mixed with foreign elements of a very disparate nature which can be grouped under the vague heading of "neo-Platonic". These are taken mainly from St. Augustine, Avicenna and Avicebron, sometimes from Proclus (*Liber de Causis*), and Averroes. The idea of a conflict between an "Augustinian philosophy" and an "Aristotelian philosophy" never entered their minds; for them, "philosophy" meant the knowledge handed down by Aristotle and the other Greek or Arab philosophers. If they foresaw any possibility of conflict, if they noticed any divergence of spirit or doctrine, it was between "philosophy" on the one hand, the work of pagan thinkers, and on the other hand the wisdom which had been scientifically worked out by theologians since the time of the Fathers, a wisdom which integrated all human sciences in its higher unity. In this wisdom, the writers prior to the thirteenth century, following the example of St. Augustine, saw philosophy in its highest sense, the philosophy of Christians.

### Eclectic Aristotelianism

Aristotelianism, then, has gained a firm foothold at Paris before 1250. It has made itself master of the Arts Faculty and has invaded the Faculty of Theology, setting up a new, more speculative, trend in opposition to the traditional trend in theology.

But this *Latin Aristotelianism* is still loosely knit, hesitant, not yet acclimatized, mixed with unassimilated suspect elements. In short, it is an *eclectic Aristotelianism* which the Latin world has not yet thought out for itself. The new disciples of the Stagirite are exegetes rather than philosophers, they are trying to penetrate the sense of the difficult texts which have come into their hands. They go for help to the paraphrases of Avicenna and more recently to the commentaries of Averroes. Without much discernment, they mix the authentic doctrine of Aristotle with neo-Platonic ideas of Jewish or Arab origin. The same characteristics mark the contemporary theological literature to the extent to which it is influenced by the philosophical movement; the writings of the theologians who are touched by the new philosophical spirit display the same eclecticism and the same hesitancies as those of the philosophers.

So the Latin philosophers of the first half of the thirteenth century take their inspiration mainly from Aristotle. But the lacunae and obscurities of Aristotle's system demand complementary doctrines to fill in the gaps and commentaries to explain the obscurities, and inevitably it is the neo-Platonic tradition which is called on to provide both. This was made even more natural by the fact that the *Liber de Causis* had long circulated under the name of Aristotle, who therefore found himself credited with the most important metaphysical theses of Proclus. We find, then, Proclus, Avicenna, Avicebron and also the Pseudo-Dionysius and St. Augustine, in turn or together, all making their contribution to the rejuvenation of peripatetic philosophy; so that Latin Aristotelianism is always in some degree and in some form a *"neo-Platonizing" Aristotelianism*. In some authors the neo-Platonic trend is so marked that it becomes dominant and one can then speak of a *Latin neo-Platonism*.

Fr. de Vaux has brought forward some traces of Avicennian influence at the beginning of the thirteenth century, and even thinks he can discern the existence of a *Latin Avicennianism*, later supplanted by Latin Averroism. It seems to us that the influence of these two trends has been exaggerated. They are secondary trends issuing from Aristotelianism and closely connected with it. As far as Avicenna's influence is concerned, we never seem to find a Latin Avicennianism properly so-called; sometimes, as in the case of Albert the Great and Roger Bacon (philosophical works), we have the neo-Platonic Aristotelianism just mentioned; sometimes we find pure neo-Platonism, as in the case of the *De Causis Primis*, where the influences of Proclus, John Scot Erigena and Avicenna are all found simultaneously. In the *De Anima* attributed to Gundissalinus, Avicenna's influence seems to be more exclusive, but even here he is only a secondary source brought in to clarify the principal source which is Aristotle. In short, we agree with M. De Wulf that there is no reason to hold that Latin Avicennianism is a distinct trend of doctrine. All that is useful in Fr. de Vaux's theory may be retained by saying that before the appearance of Averroes in the Latin world, the influence of Avicenna was outstanding in Latin Aristotelianism and neo-Platonism.

Was there, then, an Augustinian or Platonic-Augustinian school at Paris before the coming of the Aristotelianism of St. Albert and St. Thomas ? This interpretation of the intellectual evolution of the thirteenth century has been strongly criticized by M. De Wulf, and as we have seen his criticism seems en-

tirely justified. On the *philosophical plane*, Augustinianism was non-existent during the first half of the
century. The philosophical tendencies of the Arts
Faculty and the Faculty of Theology are closely akin
to one another; a basis of Aristotelian doctrine, fairly
strongly contaminated by neo-Platonic influences of
diverse origin. This doctrinal relationship between the
two faculties is quite natural, since the masters of
theology received their philosophical formation in the
Faculty of Arts. Only on the *theological plane* can
there be any question of Augustinianism among the
theologians of this period. All the characteristics of
the so-called "pre-Thomist Augustinianism" or "Platonic-Augustinian trend" really belong to the theological movement in the formal sense, and find their explanation in this fact. Thus, the more or less pronounced agreement among these masters on certain
Augustinian doctrines is simply the result of the
fact that these doctrines had long since been incorporated into western theology, where they served to
formulate certain dogmatic truths. The absence of
formal distinction between philosophy and theology,
the tendency to erase the dividing line between the
order of nature and that of grace, and finally the
tendency to make philosophy subordinate to theology
—all these are so many aspects of the attitude which
is proper to theology. For the theologian, in fact, philosophy is only an instrument to be used in the speculative method—*philosophia ancilla theologiae*. Finally, the lack of philosophical systematisation in
pre-Thomist theologians is to be explained first of
all by the eclectic nature of the philosophical world
around them, and secondly by the specific nature
of theological knowledge: the unity of the sacred

science is assured by principles which are very different from those which make for philosophical systematisation. Therefore, what links these masters together and links them to St. Augustine is the theological spirit with which they are animated, and a certain body of traditional theological doctrine. It is not
at this point directly that St. Albert and St. Thomas
will break with tradition.

So the historians who oppose the trend introduced
by St. Albert and St. Thomas to the "traditional Augustinian" trend do not realize that *the philosophico-
theological movement prior to 1250 is neither traditional nor essentially Augustinian.* It came to birth
about 1225-1230 under the influence of the new
philosophical literature which penetrated the Arts
Faculty first and then theological circles. In philosophy, Aristotle was its main inspiration, but many
secondary sources joined up with this main one,
without, however, succeeding in forming a single
homogeneous trend. In theology, these different philosophical elements blended with the traditional doctrines of Latin theology, of which St. Augustine was
the principal source. In short what is commonly called
pre-Thomist Augustinianism is *the teaching of the
Faculty of Theology, in the state at which it had
arrived about 1230 under the influence of philosophy* [1].

[1] As for *Avicennian Augustinianism* (cf. p. 31 note 1) mentioned by M. Gilson, it is still less a distinct doctrinal trend. Those
who hold this doctrine are "Christian thinkers who, under the influence of Avicenna, borrow Aristotle's terminology in order
to express the Augustinian theory of illumination". One could
hardly express more clearly the fact that it is, first, only a
*particular* doctrine, and secondly, a typical example of the
*syncretism* which is characteristic of the Latin thinkers in the
period when the new philosophical sources were being assimilated.

# CHAPTER VI

# ARISTOTELIANISM AT OXFORD
## (1200-1275)

The gradual emergence of Paris, during the thirteenth century, as the unrivalled centre of French learning was paralleled by Oxford's rise to prominence among the English schools. The origins of this old English university are still very obscure. There were schools at Oxford, teaching liberal arts and theology, from the twelfth century onwards. In 1201, John Grim bore the title of *magister scolarum Oxoniae*; while an act of 1210 refers to master Alardus as *rector scolarum*. In 1209, two or three students were unjustly executed by order of the king, and as a result the masters and students left Oxford and went to Reading, Cambridge or Paris. This *"suspendium clericorum"* of 1209 would seem to indicate the existence at that date of a sort of corporation of masters and students. In 1214, after an interruption of five years, the *studium* was reorganised by Cardinal Nicholas, the papal legate. The statute of 1214 can be considered the foundation charter of the university. From this date, the university possessed a chancellor, and it is possible or even probable that Robert Grosseteste (later bishop of Lincoln) was the first to hold this post. The Dominicans arrived in Oxford in 1221, the Franciscans joined them in 1224, and in 1229 the general strike at the university of Paris drove a great many masters and students towards Oxford. The successive influx of so many men of learning proved a decisive stimulus for the young English university. During the whole of the thirteenth century Oxford maintained close relations with Paris and came under its influence, though its own traditions were properly preserved and developed.

During the thirteenth century, England also, like Spain and Italy, became a centre for scientific translations, thanks to the initiative of Robert Grosseteste, who himself had a profound knowledge of Greek and undertook many translations [1].

## The work of Robert Grosseteste

Amid the obscurity which still surrounds the origins of the school of Oxford, one personality stands out in bold relief—that of Robert Grosseteste. He was the living incarnation of the university, the brain behind its philosophical and theological studies during the first half of the thirteenth century.

Grosseteste was born at Stradbroke in Suffolk, in 1168 at the latest, and a document written probably between 1186 and 1189 already refers to him as "*magister*". Thus he must have become a master of arts at Oxford before 1190, and there seems little doubt that he was teaching there at about that date. After being retained for some time at Hereford in the service of the bishop, William of Vere (who died in 1199), Grosseteste seems to have taught philosophy at Oxford again. This would be from 1199 to 1209,

---

[1] On the history of Oxford University, see H. RASHDALL, F. M. POWICKE, A. B. EMDEN, *The Universities of Europe in the Middle Ages*, vol. III, Oxford, 1936.

until the period of the suppression of the schools (1209-1214) and the consequent dispersal of the masters. He probably went to Paris at this time, in order to study theology. Returning to Oxford in 1214 or thereabouts, he began his career as *magister regens* in theology and became chancellor of the new university some time between 1214 and 1221. When the Franciscans arrived in 1224, he set about organizing their studies, and in 1229 or 1230 became the first *magister regens* of their *studium*. He kept this position until 1235, when he was named bishop of Lincoln; but even then he continued to take a very keen interest in the university of Oxford; he also began a translation of important Greek writings, with the help of several collaborators. He died in 1253.

In theology, Grosseteste followed the Augustinian tradition, as all his contemporaries did. To be precise, he belonged to the conservative school of Paris which Mgr. Grabmann called the "biblico-moral school". The main representatives of this school at the end of the twelfth century were Peter Comestor, Peter the Cantor and Stephen Langton. Grosseteste was true to his school in that Scripture and practical moral problems were his main interests, without much recourse to philosophy. When, as a bishop, he wrote to the theologians of Oxford, he insisted that all theological teaching should be based on texts of the Bible, and warned them not to mingle less solid materials with these scriptural foundation-stones, upon which theology has to be built. All lessons, especially the *lectiones ordinariae* in the morning, should have as their object the Old and New Testament. For, as he pointed out, this was the traditional practice of their fathers before them, besides being the custom of every *ma-*

*gister regens* in Paris, a custom which they had to uphold [1].

It does at first sight seem surprising that a conservative theologian like Grosseteste was so bold a promoter of philosophical and scientific studies at Oxford. In the *Hexaemeron*, which must date from the first years of his episcopate (not long, therefore, before he himself undertook the translation of the *Nicomachean Ethics*), we still find him severely criticizing the *"moderni qui nituntur de Aristotele haeretico facere catholicum, mira caecitate et praesumptione"*. He adds: *"Non igitur se decipiant... et Aristotelem catholicum constituendo seipsos haereticos faciant"* [2]. Like all his contemporaries, Grosseteste seems to have been subject to two divergent influences, that of tradition and that of modern trends. The influence of the latter grew stronger as the Greek and Arabic scientific literature became better known and that influence became irresistible.

At the start of his career, probably while he was teaching in the Arts Faculty (1199-1209), logic was Grosseteste's main concern. He commented on the *Sophistici Elenchi*, the *Posterior Analytics* and the *Prior Analytics*, and Fr. Callus thinks that his short *Quaestio de Substantia Rei* belongs to the same period. The glosses on the *Physics* are later. Fr. Callus suggests that they should be placed between 1230 and 1235, during the latter years of the author's teaching career; while Thomson would put them before 1229, because after that date Grosseteste devoted

---

[1] Cf. D. A. CALLUS, *The Oxford Career of Robert Grosseteste* (Oxoniensia, X, 1945).

[2] D. A. CALLUS, *The Oxford Career of Robert Grosseteste*, p. 58.

almost all his time to theology and things ecclesiastical [1].

What date must we give to the scientific and metaphysical writings of Robert Grosseteste ? Fr. Callus
does not deal with the subject in his recent works,
and these two groups of writings are not even mentioned in his study of Grosseteste's career at Oxford.
Must we therefore conclude that he would place them
all during the period of the episcopate ? According to
Thomson, Grosseteste's keen interest in the sciences
and his profound knowledge of Arabian scientific
writings probably date from his stay in Paris (about
1209-1214); his own scientific works were written
from 1214, when he began his career as a theologian,
until 1229, when he became *magister regens* of the
Franciscan *studium*. His opuscules on metaphysics
would date from the same period. As regards the truly
scientific works of Grosseteste, however, Thomson's
hypothesis is not altogether satisfactory and the learned author himself puts forward several objections;
there were scientific relationships between England
and the Arab centres in Spain as early as the twelfth
century; even at the present day there are perhaps
more twelfth and thirteenth century scientific manuscripts in English libraries than there are in Paris;
and finally, when Grosseteste was in Paris, he took an
active interest in theology and psychology. We might
therefore ask whether there are any serious reasons
why we should not attribute at least some of his
scientific works to the period before 1209, when he
was teaching *in artibus* [2].

[1] Cf. *ibid.*, p. 45-47; S. Harrison THOMSON, *The Writings of
Robert Grosseteste*, Cambridge, 1940, p. 82.
[2] Cf. S. Harrison THOMSON, *op.cit.*, p. 32-33 and 89-120.

Only after his elevation to the see of Lincoln does Grosseteste seem to have fully realized the fact that an intellectual evolution was taking place in the Christian world. Only then did he feel a desire to collaborate actively in the assimilation of pagan knowledge, without neglecting to promote the progress of theology at the same time, by the translation of eastern ecclesiastical writers.

Apart from his translations and works on logic, Grosseteste's philosophical and scientific writings might be grouped as follows:

1. Introductory scientific works: *De Utilitate Artium* and *De Generatione Sonorum* (an essay on the physiology of phonetics, of some interest as the basis of research in linguistics in the school of Robert Grosseteste).

2. Works on experimental sciences (astronomy, meteorology, cosmogony, optics, physics).

3. Works on metaphysics (*De Unica Forma Omnium, De Intelligentiis, De Statu Causarum, De Potentia et Actu*).

4. Works on ethics: Grosseteste added personal notes to his translation of the *Nicomachean Ethics*, concerning doctrine or philology. He also brought out an abridged version of the *Ethics*.

These works are of very considerable historical importance. By his scientific writings, Grosseteste became the founder of the experimental school of Oxford; the method of this school was neatly summed up by Roger Bacon in the following terms: *"Inventi enim sunt viri famosissimi, ut Robertus Lincolniensis et frater Adam de Marisco et multi alii, qui per potestatem mathematicae sciverunt causas omnium expli-*

*care et tam humana quam divina sufficienter exponere"* [1].

Besides this emphasis on the mathematical methods used in the study of natural phenomena, we must also note the part played by light in Grosseteste's scientific and even metaphysical conceptions. His theory of light serves as a link between the speculations of neo-Platonism and the natural sciences, and here also he is the founder of an important current of thought. As we have already noted, his works on phonetics and philology put him at the head of a school. And finally, it is quite evident that his translation of the *Ethics* and of the Greek commentaries on that work opened up new horizons for social and moral philosophy, as well as for moral theology.

In his philosophy, Robert was another representative of eclectic Aristotelianism. On an Aristotelian basis (logic and fundamental metaphysical doctrines) he constructed a philosophy that was greatly influenced by neo-Platonism in all its forms—Augustinian, Greek (*Liber de Causis*), Arabian (Avicenna), and Jewish (Avicebron and Isaac Israeli) [2].

## The contemporaries of Robert Grosseteste

The pages of Oxford's history during the first half of the thirteenth century are illumined for us by the brilliance of Robert Grosseteste, teacher and bishop.

---

[1] J. H. BRIDGES, *The Opus Majus of Roger Bacon*, Oxford, 1897, vol. I, . 108.

[2] The seventh centenary of Robert Grosseteste's death (1253) gave rise to many publications. The most important is the work of A. C. CROMBIE, *Robert Grosseteste and the Origins of experimental Science*, Oxford, 1953.

In fact, it is only by seeing his career as the central point that we can give even an outline sketch of the origins of the university, other evidence being so slight [1].

First, then, what was happening in the *Arts Faculty* during this period ?

While the Arts Faculty of Paris had become, through the influence of Abelard, "the most important centre for logical studies in the whole of the West", "English culture in the thirteenth century, especially in the early days before it was contaminated by the influence of the schools of Paris, was more like the culture of Chartres, enriched by the latest treasures of Arab Platonism in philosophy and science. It is not impossible that Chartres exerted a direct influence on English thought in the thirteenth century" [2]. Already towards the end of the preceding century, several English scholars could be distinguished by the use they made of the new literature in their writings. Among them were Roger of Hereford, Daniel of Morley, Alexander Neckam and Alfred of Sareshel. However, nobody has yet proved that any of them taught liberal arts at Oxford. But they were able, in any case, to exercise a doctrinal influence over the Arts Faculty at Oxford by their writings and by personal relationships.

According to Roger Bacon, St. Edmund of Abingdon was the first to "read" the *Sophistici Elenchi* at Oxford and a certain master Hughes (otherwise unknown) was the first to comment on the *Posterior*

[1] We shall be assisted in this especially by the study of D.A. CALLUS, *Introduction of Aristotelian Learning to Oxford*, London, 1943.

[2] E. GILSON, *La Philosophie au Moyen Age*, Paris, 1944, p. 469.

*Analytics.* Edmund's regency must have been from 1202 to 1209, thus coinciding with the latter years of the regency of Robert Grosseteste. If Bacon is speaking precisely, Grosseteste's commentaries on the *Organon* would come slightly after those of his two colleagues, St. Edmund and Hughes. Since the *logica nova* was not introduced earlier, it does not seem likely that the *libri naturales* were received in Oxford much earlier. According to John of Garland, his teacher John of London had taught at Oxford and had "read' the philosophers. This must have been before 1209.

John Blund, who was also a contemporary of St. Edmund, taught Arts in Paris about 1205, and at Oxford perhaps about 1207 to 1209. Henry of Avranches, writing in 1232, said of him:

Adde quod a puero studiis electus inhesit
Primus Aristotilis satagens perquirere libros,
Quando recenter eos Arabes misere Latinis,
Quos numquam fertur legisse celebrius alter
Aut prius, ut perhibent Oxonia Parisiusque [1].

It would seem, then, that Blund was one of the first to comment on the *Libri Naturales* in Paris, before the prohibition of 1210, and he seems to have been the one who introduced them at Oxford. A Cambridge manuscript contains a very interesting piece of evidence as to his teaching, namely the *Tractatus de Anima secundum Joannem Blundum.* In this, Blund quotes Plato (the *Timaeus*), Cicero, St. Augustine, Boethius and St. John Damascene, but his main sources are the Arab philosophers, Algazel and especially Avicenna, who serve as his guides in his reading of Aristotle. He shows no knowledge of Averroes,

[1] Cf. D. A. CALLUS, *op.cit.*, p. 16.

and on the whole the treatise seems to be of an early date, certainly before 1230. The work faithfully reflects the state of Latin Aristotelianism during the first thirty years of the century; Blund remains loyal to Aristotle and Avicenna, and rejects Avicebron's theories of universal hylomorphism and the plurality of forms [1].

With Adam of Buckfield, we reach the middle of the century. He was born about 1220, and was already a master of arts by 1243. In 1249 or 1250, Robert Grosseteste named him rector of the church of Iver—he was at that time a sub-deacon. He probably became a master of theology, but the only works of his that are preserved are all philosophical. He died during the episcopate of John Peckham, Archbishop of Canterbury (1279-1292). He left commentaries (*notulae, glossae*) on almost the whole of the *corpus Aristotelicum vetustius* (except the *Organon*, the *De Animalibus* and the *Ethics*), and on the *De Plantis* (pseudo-Aristotle), the *De Differentia Spiritus et Animae* of Costa ben Luca, and Avicenna's *De Caelo*. The influence of Averroes runs throughout his work and has almost as profound an influence on it as Avicenna's had on Albert the Great.

Fr. Callus distinguishes three periods in the development of Latin Aristotelianism. The first, before 1230, is the "Avicennian" period, characterized by the method of producing paraphrases in the form of autonomous treatises, each bearing the same title as the corresponding treatise of Aristotle. John Blund's *De*

---

[1] D. A. Callus observes in this connexion that these theories were thus not as "traditional" as Kilwardby and Peckham later claim. The same remark could be made concerning the school of Paris.

*Anima* is a work of this type. After 1230 comes the "Averroistic" period. Here, the characteristic method is literal commentary, *expositio per modum commenti*, which might be anything from a mere marginal gloss, or a simple analysis of the text, to a really studied commentary. It is to this period that Adam of Buckfield's works belong. The third period opens around 1275, and here we find the literal commentary giving way more and more to the *expositio per modum quaestionis*.

No doubt there are still many manuscripts hidden away in English libraries which bear witness to the scientific progress of Oxford in its early youth. Perhaps we shall receive more complete evidence about this seat of learning in the years to come.

What is there to say of the *Faculty of Theology* ?

We know the names of several theologians who were teaching at Oxford during the closing years of the twelfth century, among them being master Philip, a "fount of theological knowledge", Alexander Neckam, John Grim and Simon of Gloucester.

St. Edmund taught theology at Oxford before his elevation to the see of Canterbury in 1233. In the opinion of M. Glorieux, he left Paris (where he was a *magister regens*) in 1229 because of the strike; whereas acording to Fr. Callus he was already teaching theology at Oxford by 1222, and had probably been doing so since 1215. Thus his regency would be almost contemporary with that of Robert Grosseteste (1214-1235). We still possess some of his writings on theology and canon law.

John Blund also taught theology at Oxford, from 1229 onwards, and he died in 1248.

Robert Bacon, the friend and student companion of St. Edmund, was already a master of theology in 1219. He probably entered the Order of Preachers in 1227 and went on teaching until his death in 1248. His works have been lost [1]. Richard Fishacre was the first Dominican to become a master in Oxford (about 1240) and he taught until his death, also in 1248. Bacon and Fishacre seem to have made a very great impression on those who heard them, according to the testimony of Matthew of Paris. Fishacre was acquainted with the new literature. In his commentary on the *Sentences* (about 1240), the first to come from the pen of an English Dominican and probably the first commentary made in Oxford, he quotes Aristotle (*De Animalibus* and *De Anima* frequently, and the *Metaphysics*, book VII), Plato (the *Timaeus*), Avicenna and Averroes; he is apt to reject the opinion of Peter Lombard in favour of Aristotle, "*praecipuus ethnicorum maximorum inter philosophos*", and to compare the latter with St. Augustine, "*praecipuus inter catholicos doctores*".

Adam Marsh (de Marisco) was the first Franciscan in Oxford to be made a master. He taught at the university from 1247 or 1248 until the beginning of 1250, but his theological works have yet to be discovered. Roger Bacon praises his extensive knowledge of the natural sciences and of languages.

The Oxford theologians do not seem to have produced, during this first half-century, any monu-

---

[1] A commentary on the *Psalms*, attributed to Robert Bacon, has recently been found: cf. B. SMALLEY, *Robert Bacon and the Early Dominican School at Oxford*, in *Transactions of the Royal Historical Society*, IV[th] series, vol. XXX, 1948, p. 1-19.

mental works to compare with the great syntheses produced at Paris during the same period. For the full development of the school of Oxford we must wait till the second half of the century.

## Eclectic Aristotelianism

The traditions which Robert Grosseteste and Adam of Buckfield left behind them became stronger in the second half of the thirteenth century, and gave rise to a rather original trend in philosophy, although Paris continued to exert some influence.

In the *Arts Faculty*, the dominant figure after 1250 was Geoffrey of Aspall, who seems to have taught some time before 1265 and died in 1287. His literal commentaries on the *De Caelo*, his questions on the *Physics* and the *De Generatione* have been preserved, but his commentary on the *Metaphysics* has been lost. The work of this philosopher has not yet been studied closely and it would be difficult to sort out his main tendencies with any precision.

In the *Theological Faculty*, there seems to have been no secular master worthy of mention after the death of John Blund in 1248.

Among the Dominicans, the main theologian during this period was Robert Kilwardby, who was *magister regens* at Oxford from about 1256 to 1261. As we have already seen, he was a master of arts at Paris from 1232 to 1245 approximately, and he later became Archbishop of Canterbury (1272-1279). Although philosophy was the subject of his youth, Kilwardby turned resolutely towards the sacred science after entering the Dominican Order and was very strongly influenced by the Oxford milieu. This development is usually represented as a conversion from Aristotelianism to Augustinianism. In reality, he remained loyal, as a theologian, to the eclectic Aristotelianism which he had professed in Paris and which later seemed to him to be closely bound up with the traditional doctrines of theology. It was on behalf of this theology that, towards the end of his life, he made a stand against the innovations of Thomism.

Among the Franciscans, Adam Marsh's most outstanding successor was Thomas of York, who taught at Oxford from 1253 until about 1256. He was the author of an imposing metaphysical *summa*, the *Sapientiale*, which unfortunately is still not edited. Thomas preferred Platonism to Aristotelianism because it was nearer to the doctrine of St. Augustine, but his real masters were Avicebron and Dominic Gundisalvi; he knew William of Auvergne's *Magisterium Doctrinale* almost inside out and its influence is evident in his work. In short, the *Sapientiale* presents us with yet another shade of neo-Platonic Aristotelianism—one which has stronger leanings towards the doctrine of Avicebron. Richard Rufus succeeded Thomas of York about 1256, shortly after his return from Paris. The commentary on the *Sentences* which is attributed to him reveals a close dependence on Philip the Chancellor, John of la Rochelle, Alexander of Hales, Bonaventure, and above all Richard Fishacre. Richard quotes the great pagan philosophers, but his knowledge of Aristotle is rather superficial.

Oxford is usually credited with the production of the famous *Summa Philosophiae* edited by L. Baur. The author of this remarkable work remains hidden under the strictest anonymity [1]; it seems to have been written between 1260 and 1270. The author is more eclectic in his method than those authors whom we have so far discussed. In Paris, for example, the fundamental positions are always found to be Aristotelian, and the neo-Platonic elements are merely complementary to them; at most they add new shades of meaning to the Aristotelian doctrines. But in the eyes of our anonymous author, there is a conflict between Plato and Aristotle, and though he owes much to the latter, he does not hesitate to follow Plato on some important points such as the notion of first matter, the theory of Ideas, the existence of a spiritual matter and the theory of reminiscence. Sometimes he shows a marked antipathy towards Aristotle, especially because of his "arrogance" in discussion, although he realizes that his philosophy is safer and more scholarly than that of Plato. Moreover, our author is influenced by several other authors, modern as well as ancient—St. Augustine, Pseudo-Dionysius, Algazel, Avicebron and, nearer to his own times, Alexander of Hales, Albert the Great, perhaps Robert Grosseteste and Roger Bacon. In spite of all these, the philosophy of the *Summa* is another witness to the "progressive march of peripatetic philosophy", for Aristotelian doctrines form the main structure of the system and allow the author to integrate the various sources at his disposal into a single stream.

One last person is worthy of mention before 1275, namely John Peckham, who occupied the Franciscan

[1] Fr. Chossat thought that the *Summa Philosophiae* could be attributed to Robert Kilwardby, and Fr. Mandonnet was inclined to accept this: cf. *Bulletin Thomiste*, t. III, 1930-1933, p. 963-964.

chair at Oxford from 1271 to 1275. But we shall meet him later when we come to speak of the important part he played in Paris around 1270. Here, it will be sufficient to note that in philosophy he was an authentic representative of eclectic Aristotelianism, like his Dominican colleague Robert Kilwardby.

We could well repeat here, by way of conclusion, most of what was said above about the masters of Paris before 1250. The masters of Oxford, each in his own way (and often in ways pretty different from those adopted by their colleagues in Paris), all belonged to the great school of *neo-Platonizing and eclectic Aristotelianism* which was the first fruit of the penetration of pagan literature into the Christian West. It was only after 1277 that profound differences of opinion and dissensions in doctrine appeared in Oxford, brought on through the influence of events in Paris. They were the continuation in England of the philosophical conflicts which set one school against another in the French capital.

# CHAPTER VII

# THE DEVELOPMENT OF LATIN ARISTOTELIANISM

## (1250-1265)

The events which took place in this short period secured the triumph of philosophy and Aristotelianism at Paris. In accordance with our plan and method, we shall try to follow the stages of this rapid development, while respecting as much as possible the chronological succession of events.

### St. Bonaventure and Aristotelianism (1250-1257)

At the same time (1248) as Albert the Great left the university life of Paris, brother Bonaventure came on the scene as bachelor lecturing on the Bible. He was born in 1221, near Viterbo, and had completed his studies in the liberal arts, probably at Paris, when he entered the Friars Minor, probably in 1243. For the next two years, being stationed in their house in Paris, he was able to continue following the public lectures of John of la Rochelle and the private lessons of Alexander of Hales, both of whom died in 1245. From 1245 to 1248, he sat at the feet of Eudes Rigaud, *magister regens* of the Franciscan school. In 1248 he became bachelor in Biblical studies, and in 1250 began his lectures on the *Sentences* as bachelor; he proceeded as master about 1253, and occupied the Franciscan chair from 1253 to 1257. On February 2nd, 1257, he was elected minister general of the Franciscan order. From this moment, he was practically lost to scientific work, his absorbing occupations as head of the order leaving him scarcely any leisure for regular study. But he continued to take an active interest in the evolution of ideas, and intervened strongly in the doctrinal struggles provoked by the progress of Aristotelianism. He died at Lyons, after the close of the Council there, on July 15th, 1274, at the age of fifty-three.

The problem that faces us now is to decide what was Bonaventure's attitude to Aristotelianism during his teaching years, from 1248 to 1257. We may say at once that we cannot accept all the views expressed by M. Gilson in his book, *La Philosophie de Saint Bonaventure*. In this work—which is so justly famous and has become almost a classic—M. Gilson seems to have reacted excessively against the judgment which the scholarly Franciscan editors of Quaracchi have passed on the work of the Doctor Seraphicus. We may allow that the editors wanted to bring their views into line with those expressed by Leo XIII in his encyclical in favour of Thomism; perhaps they went too far in this direction; but surely this tendency did not reach the proportions attributed to it today, nor would it notably falsify the historical perspective of such scholars.

It is quite true that the *Commentary on the Sentences* is a youthful work—as were indeed most works of this kind. Bonaventure wrote it when he was thirty, at the very beginning of a theological career which might well have extended over many years. Such a literary monument, composed at the first

attempt, brings out in full relief the exceptional gifts
of the author; but it also justifies the regret expressed
by the editors of Quaracchi that such an academic
career should have been cut short prematurely; and
it is of these expressions of regret that M. Gilson seems
to disapprove.

It is also true to say that St. Bonaventure wrote
this great work at a time when the assimilation of
Aristotle was not yet completed, and before new life
was brought to philosophical and theological studies
by Albert the Great and Thomas Aquinas. Concerning Albert's influence on Bonaventure, M. Gilson
writes: "Whether Bonaventure did or did not actually
attend his lectures, it is highly unlikely that in such
a restricted world as the university of Paris he should
have remained ignorant of Albert's teaching; especially a teaching of such enterprise and audacity as
to separate philosophy from theology; to base the
proofs for the existence of God solidly on the facts
of experience; and to refuse to accept that creation
of the world in time was demonstrable by reason...
It was not therefore ignorance of Albert the Great's
Aristotelian reform which made Bonaventure refuse
to follow this route". Does that really correspond to
the historical facts ? If we turn back to the preceding
pages where we described Albert's teaching in Paris,
it will be seen that his "enterprise and audacity" and
his "Aristotelian reform" are still a thing of the
future: St. Bonaventure could hardly react against an
innovation which had not yet started. Moreover, it is
certainly not correct to say that Albert refused "to
accept that the creation of the world in time was
demonstrable by reason"; on the contrary, he shares
St. Bonaventure's views on this point.

M. Gilson also exaggerates Bonaventure's acquaintance with the works of Aristotle. His studies *in artibus* took place about 1240—at a time when, as we have seen, little more of Aristotle was taught than the *Organon* and the first three books of the *Ethics*; at the most he may have been there at the beginning of Roger Bacon's period and thus heard his lectures on the *Physics* and *Metaphysics*. He may have read Aristotle for himself, but he speaks of him in a way that suggests a rather superficial knowledge of his metaphysical doctrines, as we shall soon show.

In order to form a clear idea of St. Bonaventure's attitude to Aristotle and the pagan philosophers during his teaching years, we ourselves have made an enquiry directly on the subject; the method was to take a certain number of soundings in the places where one would expect him to come to grips with the main errors of paganism and the characteristic doctrines of the philosophers [1]. The results went far beyond the immediate object we had in mind, and they enable us to draw a very clear picture of St. Bonaventure's attitude in the *Commentary on the Sentences*.

He has a fairly extensive knowledge of Aristotle's works, and he quotes other philosophers also, Averroes among them. No doubt he owes his philosophical initiation to the Faculty of Arts, but he probably borrows a fair number of his quotations from his predecessors. In any case, his knowledge of pagan philosophy is not deep, and he is fully conscious of the fact: he declares himself incompetent to settle disputed questions of Aristotelian exegesis, and often shows a cer-

[1] Cf. F. Van Steenberghen, *Siger de Brabant d'après ses œuvres inédites*, pp. 449-456.

tain reserve in his comments on opinions attributed
to the philosophers [1].

St. Bonaventure is a professor of theology, and has
an exalted conception of the sacred science, its transcendence, its own particular methods, its religious and
moral object. Since the first principles of theological
knowledge are revealed truths, the theologian judges
all human opinions in the light of the rule of faith,
and accepts them only in so far as they agree with
the *veritas catholica*. In virtue of this method, Bonaventure rejects any philosophical conception which
he judges to be incompatible with the traditional
theological teaching in matters concerning faith [2].

St. Bonaventure is convinced of the weakness of
human reason left to its own lights, and is not surprised at the errors of pagan philosophy: they were
inevitable, crude and harmful as they sometimes are,
without the help of revelation. Thus, one must give
much more credit to the teaching of the faith than
to the opinions of the pagan philosophers [3].

On the other hand, philosophy is a valuable auxil-
iary science of theology. By philosophy, Bonaventure
means the acquisition of knowledge by the human

[1] The texts themselves do not support M. Gilson when he
expresses opinions such as: "From the first moment that he
came into contact with Aristotle's pagan thought, St. Bonaventure thought that he had understood, judged, and passed beyond
it"; "he knows Aristotle very well...»; «he knows both sides of
the question and opts resolutely for tradition".

[2] In this attitude he is at one with all orthodox theologians,
St. Albert and St. Thomas, as well as William of Auvergne and
Alexander of Hales.

[3] This again is an attitude common to all orthodox theologians.
We need only mention the famous passage of St. Thomas in the
*Summa contra Gentiles* (I, 3-8), on the moral necessity of re-
velation.

reason, as was effected by pagan thinkers outside of Christianity, and by the Faculty of Arts in his time. St. Bonaventure's *Sentences* contain not even a hint of condemnation of philosophical research; on the contrary, the philosophers are consulted in anything which has to do with their speculation, and when their findings agree with the teaching of the Church, he is only too willing to add their authority to that of the Fathers and Doctors of the faith.

His attitude towards Aristotle shows neither mistrust, nor hostility, nor condemnation, but only esteem, respect and sympathy. As far as possible, he avoids opposing Aristotelianism to orthodox Christianity or the thought of St. Augustine. He pushes the favourable interpretation of Aristotle to the utmost, and when his errors are undeniable, even tries to excuse them [1].

Finally, we may note how the moral and religious qualities of the saint continually show through in his work; he is completely imbued with faith, piety, modesty and charity, opposed to heated controversy and sterile dispute.

Can we now sum up St. Bonaventure's doctrinal po-

[1] We find it therefore quite impossible to subscribe to M. Gilson's judgment on this matter: in the *Sentences*, "to the Seraphic Doctor, Aristotelianism is a condemned doctrine"; "Aristotelianism is not an advance which he is unaware of, but an error which he condemns"; "it is with first-hand knowledge that he opts resolutely for tradition"; "here are two different metaphysical systems meeting head-on, not an uncertain doctrine hesitating timidly before something it does not know" (p. 16). All these statements seem to us seriously inaccurate. They are all the more inaccurate if they are intended to serve as a basis for opposing St. Bonaventure's attitude to that of St. Thomas.

sition in regard to the principal errors of pagan philosophy ?

In metaphysics, he opposes all philosophical conceptions incompatible with the Christian doctrine of creation—aseity of matter, eternity of the world, creation by intermediaries or progressive emanation, denial of providence. The universe in its entirety is the immediate term of creative causality: God is the exemplary cause of the created world, and He governs it by His providence: an "eternal creation" is a contradiction in terms. On this last point, S. Bonaventure's position is very different from that of St. Thomas, and his main argument against the eternalist thesis is extremely weak.

In physics, Bonaventure rejects astrological determinism; the influence of the heavenly bodies on the sublunary world is very extensive, but it leaves intact man's spiritual activity.

In psychology, he naturally condemns Averroistic monopsychism, and refutes several of the Averroistic arguments quite satisfactorily. But he does not meet the essential difficulty of Averroes, concerning the multiplicity of spiritual human souls. His ignorance of the exigencies of Aristotelian metaphysics on this point prevents him from seeing the acuteness of the problem; since his criticism, then, is not based on principles admitted by the Aristotelians, it can neither satisfy nor refute them.

St. Bonaventure's general position in relation to the errors of pagan philosophy may be compared to that of St. Thomas, briefly, as follows. On the whole, the teaching of the two coincides, because it coincides with the traditional Christian teaching. On the whole, also, the method of argument used by St. Bonaventure is the same as that found in the later works of St. Thomas, although St. Thomas's argumentation is at once wider and deeper. But on two essential points their attitude differs: namely, the duration of the created world and the individuation of human souls. On the first point, St. Bonaventure opposes the views of the philosophers with an imaginative conception of *creatio ex nihilo,* and his refutation of the eternalist thesis, in so far as it rests on this conception, is completely ineffectual. On the second point, the individuation of souls, he puts forward his own view along with the Aristotelian; but he does not attempt to come to grips with the latter, and therefore never refutes it. St. Thomas's tactics are quite different: he meets his adversaries on the common ground of Aristotelian principles and insists on answering their objections according to these principles.

One more question must be raised concerning St. Bonaventure's *Sentences*: does this work contain a philosophy, and if so, how should it be described? Here we must touch on the famous controversy between M. Gilson and Fr. Mandonnet.

In his book on St. Bonaventure's philosophy, M. Gilson had expressed original and often penetrating views on the thought of the Seraphic Doctor. Thus, for St. Bonaventure philosophy is one element of total Christian wisdom, or, better, it is one of the steps by which the Christian intelligence rises from the obscurities of faith to the full clarity of the Beatific Vision: human knowledge or philosophy, sacred science or theology, the light of the gifts of the Holy Ghost or mystical contemplation—these are all so many successive steps in the ascent of the Christian intellectual life. M. Gilson declares that contemporary historians are disconcerted by Bonaventure's philosophy, because they have become accustomed to the modern idea of philosophy, understood as a purely rational knowledge, autonomous with regard to faith. They feel a certain lack of cohesion, because they have not discovered the central point which gives unity to this philosophy. This central point is Christ; to possess Christ is supreme wisdom, and "the purpose of philosophy is to enable us to attain this centre". St. Bonaventure conforms to the specifically Augustinian method of philosophizing, and thus achieves such a close collaboration between rational reflexion, theology and mysticism, that it is impossible to distinguish the different levels of knowledge integrated in this synthesis, this "metaphysic of Christian mysticism". "If philosophy means pure reason, then there is no philosophy in St. Bonaventure", for he rejects the rationalistic conception of philosophy. "It is correct to say that St. Bonaventure's teaching admits a formal distinction between philosophy and theology; · but after positing the distinction as real, he denies it as being unlawful"; he "positively condemns this distinction"; "St. Bonaventure was not unaware of it; he was aware of it, but did not agree with it"; his philosophy is a "heteronomous science", he "puts it into a context of supernatural ideas and influences which transform it", and "we find a transmutation of philosophical values". In a word, St. Bonaventure achieved the "mystical synthesis of medieval Augustinianism", just as St. Thomas was the author of "Christian Aristotelianism". Thus, "St. Bonaventure's teaching ... cannot strictly be compared with that of St. Thomas at any point".

So far M. Gilson. Now, in his *Siger de Brabant*, Fr. Mandonnet had already stressed the fact that the "Augustinian theologians" of the thirteenth century did not distinguish clearly between the realm of philosophy and that of theology. Nevertheless, he differed from M. De Wulf in holding that there was a "philosophical link" connecting these thinkers together—"a series of more or less clearly defined Platonic theses"; and therefore, Fr. Mandonnet concluded, it would be illogical to suppress them in the history of philosophy, unless one were to suppress at the same time all systems which were a syncretism of philosophy and religion—beginning with Platonism and neo-Platonism.

In 1926, in a critical review of M. Gilson's work on St. Bonaventure, Fr. Mandonnet first of all conceded that the editors of Quaracchi had made a regrettable attempt to harmonise St. Bonaventure and St. Thomas, whereas there are in fact profound differences between them. But he excused this move by crediting it to their perspicacity: "They held certain of St. Bonaventure's positions to be untenable; and if they were to present these perplexing doctrines without attenuation, it might bring out St. Bonaventure's individualism, but the net result would be a loss". As for M. Gilson's central thesis, Fr. Mandonnet claimed that under the title of "St. Bonaventure's philosophy", he had presented a theological and mystical synthesis. According to Gilson himself, Bonaventure had condemned the formal distinction between philosophy and theology; how, then, could we speak of his "philosophical system"? For Bonaventure, philosophy is only an instrument of theology, and therefore he is a theologian, but not a philosopher.

This interesting debate was the prelude to subsequent controversies on Christian philosophy, with particular reference to the interpretation of medieval thought. In our opinion, the disagreement between M. Gilson and Fr. Mandonnet could easily be settled by making the necessary distinctions and definitions, and thus eliminating what is too exclusively one-sided in either position.

We will leave aside, provisionally, the later works of St. Bonaventure; their teaching is not very different from that of the *Sentences*, but the atmosphere is quite different, and could put us off the track. As far as the *Sentences* is concerned, his position is quite clear. He is writing a *theological* synthesis, and is well aware of it; much of his procedure can be explained and justified only by this fact; at every step, he gives preference to such or such a philosophical opinion because it agrees better with Scripture, or with the Fathers or Doctors of the faith; a method which is quite legitimate in theology, but is meaningless in philosophy. In his *Sentences*, then, Bonaventure is formally a theologian, exactly as is Alexander of Hales in his *Summa Theologica* and St. Thomas in his. None of these masters ever pretended to be writing a "Christian philosophy", or to be putting this "Christian philosophy" in opposition to that practised in the Faculty of Arts. But they all used philosophy as an instrument of theological speculation, and in order to do this, they had to have philosophical ideas. And since St. Bonaventure never wrote any philosophical works, we are reduced to delving into his theological writings in search of his philosophical opinions. Even if the author had condemned all distinction between philosophy and theology, such an enquiry would still be lawful; for the historian could distinguish, in the works of the theologian, between what is *received* by Revelation, and what is *established* by reason. But St. Bonaventure does not actually go as far as that. He does not condemn the distinction between philosophy and theology; on the contrary, it is presupposed all through his *Commentary on the Sentences*, since among his sources he constantly distinguishes between the *sancti* and the *philosophi*[1]. He only condemns the errors of pagan philosophers, and he notes that these are due to the fact that they do not have the light of faith; this implies that Christian philosophers have the advantage of being forewarned against certain errors by the teaching of the faith, on condition, of course, that they pay attention to the directions of Christian teaching in working out their system.

Now it is precisely at this point that the problem of the relations between faith and reason is raised: how can philosophy remain faithful to its principles and method, while accepting the control of Revelation? This problem does not seem to have occupied St. Bonaventure's attention, and there is no doubt that it is one of the weaknesses of his position. Dominated as he was by the point of view of faith and theology, he does not seem to have seen the necessity, even from this point of view, of guaranteeing the autonomy of philosophical research.

This weakness lays bare another, one that is still more serious. The *Commentary on the Sentences* is the work of an exceptionally gifted mind; his clarity

[1] Later, at the time of the struggle against heterodox philosophy, he does condemn the use of philosophy which takes no account of the rule of faith; but St. Thomas does so just as strongly, notably in his *De Unitate Intellectus*, at the end.

of thought, so methodical and precise, reveals a sin-
gular aptitude for philosophy; but circumstances
diverted him from specifically philosophical research,
and he did not sufficiently think out philosophical
problems *for their own sakes*. The unity of his
thought is certainly not a philosophical unity—on this
most important point both M. Gilson and Fr. Mandonnet are in complete agreement. The former is
obliged to recognize the fact that there is no rational
synthesis in St. Bonaventure and to propose Christ as
the central point in his system. The latter notes that
the synthesis achieved by St. Bonaventure is a theological one, and that the nature of the philosophical elements incorporated in it and the part they are called
on to play can only be justified if looked at from a
theological point of view.

St. Bonaventure's "heteronomous philosophy" is
nothing else than his theological speculation, that is
to say, the use of philosophical themes in the interpretation of revealed doctrine. The philosophy which St.
Thomas incorporates in his *Summa Theologiae* is quite
as heteronomous as that of St. Bonaventure. But the
difference between the two lies in this: St. Thomas
had meditated deeply on philosophical problems and
had carved out a solid system of philosophy before
using it in theology; while St. Bonaventure did not
do this to the same extent [1].

[1] No doubt the most typical example of St. Bonaventure's
inferiority in philosophy is in the question of the existence of
God. In the *Sentences*, the problem is treated in summary fashion,
although there was an obvious occasion to treat it fully. He
claims that the existence of God is evident; M. Gilson has shown
that this opinion is due to "the Franciscan sentiment of God's
presence in nature", and to the affirmation of an intimate religious experience which is connatural to us. But all this is

We should not conclude that the Seraphic Doctor is not a philosopher, and that his work is of no interest in the history of philosophy. He has numerous and sometimes very original philosophical opinions, and these made a notable contribution to the development of thought in the thirteenth century, and particularly of Aristotelianism. But it must be admitted that he had neither the time nor, perhaps, the interest to elaborate a strict philosophical synthesis. His philosophical ideas still suffered from a troublesome eclecticism, similar to that which affected all his contemporaries, philosophers as well as speculative theologians.

To sum up: we think that M. Gilson was wrong to present as "St. Bonaventure's philosophy" a mutilated [1] exposition of his theology; but that, on the other hand, Fr. Mandonnet has minimised the philosophical importance of St. Bonaventure's work.

What conclusions are we to draw from this discussion ? We must conclude that it is difficult to describe Bonaventure's "philosophy", just as it is to describe that of William of Auvergne or Alexander of Hales. A mere glance at his philosophical doctrines shows this clearly. His basic positions are genuinely *Aristotelian*: the logic, the doctrine of abstraction (including the affirmation of a personal active intellect which is the active principle of knowledge), the essential metaphysical theses (act and potency, matter and form, substance and accidents), the physical and biological

gratuitous and rather confused; such a solution to the problem does not answer the very legitimate critical demands of reason.

[1] Mutilated, because it ignores all the *exclusively theological elements* — Trinity, Incarnation, Redemption, Grace, etc.

ideas, the notions of moral philosophy—in short, an exceedingly large part of the philosophy bequeathed to the world by Aristotle has been inherited by Bonaventure. But, following the example of his predecessors and contemporaries, he eliminates certain Aristotelian doctrines as incompatible with Catholic doctrine, and, on the other hand, tries to complete Aristotelianism in various directions. The choice of these complementary elements is often dictated by theological motives, without sufficient regard for the rational cohesion of the system. Thus, the neo-Platonic doctrine of illumination is put side by side with the doctrine of abstraction; Aristotle's hylomorphic doctrine undergoes various adaptations which betray the influence of Avicebron (for example in the idea of spiritual matter, or plurality of forms), and of St. Augustine (in the *rationes seminales*); in the study of God, the Aristotelian lines of thought are pushed into the background to make way for the traditional conceptions of Latin theology (as found in Augustine, Anselm, and Richard of St. Victor) or the ideas of Pseudo-Dionysius; in psychology, the hylomorphic view of human nature is replaced by a doctrine which uneasily preserves the unity of man, and which aggravates the Augustinian dualism by expressing it in Aristotelian terminology.

Taking everything into account, we can say that we have here once more a *neo-Platonizing Aristotelianism*, in which elements of varied origins come together without really blending. On the *philosophical* plane, we can only speak of Bonaventure's *Augustinianism* if we are prepared to juggle arbitrarily with historical facts. It is as a *theologian*, and only as such, by the spirit of his theology and by its principal doctrines, that St. Bonaventure belongs to the Augustinian school, or to the *Augustinian trend in theology*. In philosophy, St. Augustine is one of the sources of his thought, but is secondary with respect to Aristotelianism. In short, St. Bonaventure's philosophy is an *eclectic Aristotelianism with neo-Platonic tendencies, put at the service of an Augustinian theology*.

St. Bonaventure, then, is a further witness to the growing hold that Aristotelianism was gaining in Paris. His philosophical training is essentially due to Aristotle, and he recognizes him as the greatest of the pagan philosophers. But he is dealing with the sacred science, and therefore philosophy is not uppermost in his mind. In fact, as far as the speculative method is concerned, we can even say that his *Commentary on the Sentences* marks a decline, and a tendency to return to the old, more specifically theological methods of scriptural and patristic theology. St. Bonaventure has achieved a remarkable synthesis of traditional theology, but he is not one of the advance-guard of philosophical progress.

## The Arts Faculty of Paris

In 1252, while brother Bonaventure was pursuing his task as bachelor lecturing on the *Sentences* in the Franciscan school, a conflict broke out between the secular masters and the Dominicans. This struggle had been latent for many years, and it quickly degenerated into a bitter quarrel between the seculars and the regulars, since the Franciscans made common cause with the Dominicans in defence of the rights they had acquired. Soon the conflict moved into the doctrinal field, when William of St. Amour, in 1255, attacked the religious state and the mendicant way of life in his theological pamphlet, *De Periculis Novissimorum Temporum*.

The Faculty of Arts was not concerned directly in the struggle and played only a secondary part in it. But it was during those stormy years that the legal acceptance of Aristotle was definitely achieved.

The year 1252 is an important date in the history of Aristotelianism at Paris. We know that the Arts Faculty was composed of four "nations" or corporate groups of masters and students. These organizations linked together the university members who came from the same province or country (Picardy, France, Normandy, England); those who did not belong to any of these regions were affiliated to one or other of the four "nations", which enjoyed certain rights and a certain administrative autonomy. Now, at the very beginning of 1252, sometime before February 16th, the English "nation" promulgated new statutes regulating the admission of bachelors to the degree of master, and at the same time specified the subjects for the examination. These statutes made it obligatory for candidates to the *licentia docendi* to have attended lectures on the *Logica Vetus* and *Logica Nova*, on the *Liber Sex Principiorum*, the *Priscianus Minor*, the *Priscianus Magnus* and the *Barbarismus*; and, in addition, on Aristotle's *Liber de Anima*.

It is rather strange that the new rule does not mention other works of Aristotle. For example, the omission of the *Ethics* is surprising in the light of what we already know; the statutes of 1215 authorized the reading of it, and the philosophical literature prior to 1250 includes several commentaries on it. It must be concluded that the teaching of the *Ethics* remained optional, in conformity with the directives of 1215. We are also surprised not to find Aristotle's *Libri Naturales* mentioned in the curriculum, since Roger Bacon, a member of the English nation, had been lecturing on them for many years. Here again, we must presume that the teaching of these books, which were not covered by the act of 1215, was not obligatory. But these facts only make the introduction of the *De Anima* more significant. It shows that the masters of this period attached very great importance to the study of psychology and, it may be presumed, especially to the study of the intellect; this would be because the doctrine of abstraction and the explanation of intellectual activity were closely connected with the problems of dialectics, speculative grammar, and even morality. But whatever the origin or motive of the measures taken in 1252, this is the first official transgression of the ecclesiastical prohibitions which had attached to the *Libri Naturales* of Aristotle and the pagan commentaries on them since 1210; and it was fraught with serious consequences. Aristotle's *De Anima* paves the way for the commentary of Averroes, and the latter was to open the eyes of the Arts Faculty to a whole world of problems and difficulties of which they had not till then suspected the existence. Many were so won over by the skilful dialectic of Averroes that they followed him even in his most pernicious doctrines.

However, the initiative taken by the English nation in 1252 was only a prelude, and was followed, on March 19th, 1255, by a more general and more comprehensive measure. This date marks the final step towards the complete acceptance of Aristotle by the Arts Faculty. For on this date an act was promulgated, by the whole faculty this time, reorganizing the studies and putting all known works of Aristotle on the curriculum, including three Aristotelian pseudepigraphs, the *De Causis*, the *De Plantis* and the *De Differentia Spiritus et Animae*. Besides the *Logica Vetus* and *Logica Nova*, with the classical commentaries of Boethius, and besides the works on grammar and the *Sex Principia*, the following works are mentioned: *ethicas quantum ad quatuor libros* (that is, the *Ethica Vetus* and the *Ethica Nova*), *physicam Aristotelis, metaphysicam et librum de animalibus, librum celi et mundi, librum primum metheorum, librum de anima, librum de generatione, librum de causis, librum de sensu et sensato, librum de sompno et vigilia, librum de plantis, librum de memoria et reminiscentia, librum de differentia spiritus et animae* (by Costa ben Luca), *librum de morte et vita*.

The notes and conditions embodied in the text make it clear that it is not introducing a program of lectures which had been unknown until then, but that it is legalizing and making obligatory a situation which had been in existence for some time. No doubt that was why the acts of 1252 and 1255 did not arouse any protest from the bishop or the theologians or the Pope; the ban on Aristotle had been a dead letter for as long as ten years, perhaps, and no one at Paris thought of reviving it.

The new rule was intended to assure better organization and better coordination in the course, and to suppress the vagaries of private initiative which had abused the liberty of the system. For this purpose it imposed a clearly-defined timetable and program of studies.

And now, Aristotle is master of the house. The old school of liberal arts had long been a very active centre of dialectical and grammatical studies; from now on it was to be a centre of philosophical research in the widest sense of the term. Having been so long debarred from the study of natural philosophy and metaphysics, the members of the Arts Faculty set to work with all the more zeal in order to make up for lost time. The seed sown by the act of March 19th, 1255 falls on fertile ground; and from it springs forth heterodox Aristotelianism.

In order to understand the origins of this movement, it would be useful to know in detail the teaching of the Arts Faculty between 1250 and 1265; to know the names and work of the masters who introduced the adherents of radical Aristotelianism to philosophy—the masters of Siger of Brabant, Boetius of Dacia, Bernier of Nivelles and the others. Unfortunately, we are faced with an almost complete blank, apart from the work of Nicholas of Paris, who may have been Siger's professor of logic. The professorial activity of Nicholas seems to have extended over many years, for his name figures in two documents, one of which is dated 1254 and the other 1263. But as far as natural philosophy is concerned, the manuscript sources are still untapped, and one of the main tasks of the near future must be to try to unseal them. As far as we know, the only manuscript so far brought to the attention of scholars is the treatise *De Principiis Naturae*, written in 1256 by master John of Sicca Villa, master of arts and rector of the university at that time. If we are to believe Roger Bacon, the masters of the Arts Faculty did not publish anything during this period, so all we can expect to find will be notes of their oral teaching.

## The work of Albert the Great

During the last years of his stay in Paris, that is to say from 1245 to 1248, Albert the Great had included among his audience the young Thomas Aquinas, who had been a Dominican novice since 1244. Thomas followed his master to Cologne and attended his lectures there from 1248 to 1252. The six years that Albert spent at Cologne (1248-1254) before his appointment as provincial (1254-1257) were taken up with the organization of the new *studium generale* and with the teaching of theology. At this time Albert seems to have been absorbed by the neo-Platonic mysticism of Pseudo-Dionysius, and wrote long commentaries on all his works. There can be no doubt that this exposition of the principal themes of neo-Platonism had a great effect on the mind of his gifted disciple. In addition, however, Albert also inaugurated lectures on philosophy at the *Studium* in Cologne; Mgr. Pelzer has found three copies of his course on the *Nicomachean Ethics*, arranged from the notes of Thomas Aquinas.

In all probability, this was Albert's first philosophical work. It is devoted to problems of moral philosophy, and is thus still connected with his theological preoccupations. From this moment, however, he seems to have had a clear insight into the intellectual needs of his times, and is definitely won over to the cause of philosophy, in spite of meeting with some opposition inside his own order. In his commentary *In*

*Epistolas Beati Dionysii Areopagitae,* indeed, an annoyance that had been too long pent up breaks forth with a violence of expression that surprises us today: "Some people who know no better oppose the use of philosophy with every means in their power, especially in the Dominican Order, where there is no one to withstand them. Like brute beasts, they blaspheme what they do not understand" [1].

A rather annoying ambiguity surrounds this famous text, for the sense can vary according as we make *maxime in Praedicatoribus* agree with *Quidam* or with *usum philosophiae.* In the first case, it would mean that the adversaries of philosophy were to be found especially among the Dominicans, and Albert is assailing the obscurantism which rules inside the order [2]; in the second case, the adversaries of philosophy do not belong to the order, but they reproach especially the Dominicans for their interest in profane learning, and the latter were wrong in not resisting these attacks. Both interpretations seem equally defensible. The second has the advantage that it supresses the slightly shocking and rather unlikely invective against his own *confrères*; it has the support of interesting texts which show that the Dominicans were in fact

[1] "*Quamvis quidam qui nesciunt, omnibus modis volunt impugnare usum philosophiae, et maxime in Praedicatoribus, ubi nullus eis resistit, tamquam bruta animalia blasphemantes in iis quae ignorant*" (Vivès, t. XIV, p. 910).

[2] This is the interpretation taken by M. M. Gorce. As usual, it is expressed in a surprising style: "He (Albert) was complaining of those of his *confrères* who did not realize the importance of science and philosophy. He called them "beasts" and declared that they were too numerous. But to the better-intentioned of these "beasts" he taught good lessons suited to their mentality". Cf. M. M. GORCE, *L'essor de la pensée au moyen âge,* Paris, 1933, p. 120.

reproached for their interest in philosophy, especially during the quarrel between the seculars and regulars. But the first interpretation also has the support of texts; Fr. Mandonnet himself has provided documentation which shows that there was serious opposition to philosophy inside the order itself, in compliance with the directives formulated in the Constitutions of 1228. Thus, in 1230, two Dominican preachers (one of them John of St. Giles, the *magister regens* in theology who had recently entered the house of St.Jacques) put theologians on their guard against the abuse of philosophy and the excessive cult of Aristotle, and do not mince their terms in doing so. Humbert of Romans, the fifth master-general of the order (from 1254 to 1263), speaks in a way which suggests that he is counteracting an unfavourable attitude to profane studies. In his *Vitae Fratrum*, written in 1262, Gerard of Frachet again condemns certain religious who display an inordinate attachment to philosophy and study. And finally, Vincent of Beauvais, in his *Speculum*, excuses himself for having given so much time to natural science, metaphysics, and especially medicine: *"quia professionem meam non decuit hujuscemodi rebus investigandis ac describendis tam diligenter insistere"*, he writes concerning medical questions.

However, whichever interpretation is correct, Albert certainly complains of the failure of the order to react against the enemies of philosophy: *ubi nullus eis resistit*. Fr. Mandonnet remarks elsewhere: "It is curious to note a sort of bifurcation in the career of many famous Dominicans (men like Vincent of Beauvais, Robert Kilwardby and Thomas of Cantimpré) and also in one of the first Franciscans of Paris, John of la Rochelle. Either they finish by abandoning learning, as did Cantimpré, or at least by attenuating their expressions of admiration for it, as in the case of Vincent of Beauvais; or else they return more or less spontaneously to Augustinianism, as did Kilwardby and John of la Rochelle".

Albert, then, was convinced of the importance of profane knowledge, and it was he who definitely committed his order to scientific research and philosophical study; so definitely indeed that the General Chapters of 1271, 1278 and 1280 will react and remind the friars of the primacy of theology. Albert was assisted in his efforts by the master-general of whom we have just spoken, Humbert of Romans. He contributed largely to the progress of profane learning in the order; he commented on the chapter relating to studies in the Constitutions of 1228 in such a way as to make the exception there provided for practically equivalent to a general rule, so numerous were the reasons which made the reading of philosophical works useful and lawful: "*fidei defensio, destructio errorum philosophorum, intelligentia Scripturarum, fidei corroboratio, acuitio ingenii ad scindendum parietem Sacrae Scripturae, virtus motiva, proprii ministerii honorificatio, philosophicae scientiae contemptus*".

While he was provincial of Germany (1254-1257), Albert made a short stay at the Papal curia. The General Chapter of 1256 was held in Paris at Pentecost, when the struggle between seculars and regulars reached its climax. The master-general met Albert here, and sent him to Alexander IV to defend the cause of the mendicants. During this period at the curia, Albert was commanded by the Pope to refute the errors of Averroes concerning the personal immortality of man. This task gave rise to the little treatise *De Unitate Intellectus contra Averroem*; much later, some time after 1270, Albert modified this work in several important particulars and inserted it into his *Summa Theologica*. The opuscule against the unicity of the intellect is valuable evidence of the mental attitude which was predominant in 1256. Fr. Salman has studied the exact scope of the book and we will retail and discuss his conclusions here.

The *De Unitate* is not, as has been claimed, the redaction of a public dispute which took place in the presence of the Pope, between Albert and the adherents of Averroistic monopsychism.

Was the Pope's request motivated by the need to silence declared Averroists ? It seems not. The monopsychism of Averroes had only recently been discovered by Christian philosophers; for curiously enough, this most important doctrine of Averroes had long ·escaped the notice of Latin readers. In his *Quaestiones supra Libros Primae Philosophiae* and in his *Quaestiones supra Librum de Causis*, Roger Bacon credits Averroes with the doctrine of multiplicity of possible and active intellects. Albert the Great similarly, in his *Summa de Creaturis*, thinks that in teaching the multiplicity of active intellects he is on the side of Averroes as against all the other interpreters of Aristotle; and the English commentator, Adam of Buckfield, contemporary with the two just mentioned, reads Averroes in much the same way. From this it is clear that before 1250 the influence of Averroes was by no means in the direction of monopsychism, but on the contrary was in favour of the doctrinal position held by Albert the Great and Thomas Aquinas. At the moment when Alexander IV made his request to Albert, the real position of Averroes had become known, and the Pope invited him to oppose it; nevertheless, the analysis of the opuscule shows that it is not a question of refuting a heresy which was wide-spread throughout the Christian world, but only of settling a knotty point of philosophy which had raised difficulties in the minds of some Christian philosophers [1]. The problem was a fundamental one from the religious point of view, since it involved personal immortality; the Pope therefore took advantage of Albert's presence to obtain a scientific solution to it. It is quite probable that Albert's exposition was the theme of a solemn conference in the presence of the Papal court, and that the definitive redaction of the text in view of publication was only completed later.

The author clearly defines the problem to be treated: it is the *personal* immortality of the human soul: is it, or is it not, true to say that what remains of one individual soul after death is distinct from what remains of another ? Albert brings up thirty arguments against personal immortality; and a careful examination of these arguments shows that he is

[1] Our minds turn naturally to Paris, where the influence of pagan thinkers had been considerable since the beginning of the century, and where that of Averroes must have increased rapidly since the statute of 1252. In 1256, moreover, the Pope was occupied with the affairs of the university of Paris. Nevertheless, we must not forget that there was another place which was susceptible to Arab influence — the university of Naples. The Pope may well have been disturbed by tendencies in the philosophical teaching there.

aiming at the whole of Arabianism, not just Averroes; only four of the arguments are from Averroes. The same conclusion appears from the examination of the arguments in favour of personal immortality—Averroes is not the only, nor even the principal, adversary aimed at.

The *De Unitate Intellectus contra Averroem*, then, should not put us on the wrong track. It reveals a certain uneasiness in the philosophical world in 1256, but it does not by any means indicate Latin Averroism. Fr. Salman writes of the *De Unitate*: "So far from revealing the existence of Averroist agitation, it shows that Averroes's influence was still very restricted, submerged in a confused mass of doctrinal influences which can only be called *Arabianism*... If by "Latin Averroism" is meant a synthesis made by Christian thinkers who base themselves on Averroes's general doctrine and develop it in their own way, then this heresy was not in existence in 1256". We may also note that it is highly unlikely that such a flagrant and pernicious heresy as monopsychism should have been taught in a Christian country since about 1250, and provoked the intervention of ecclesiastical authority only twenty years later.

We will not pause to discuss the philosophical value of the opuscule. Mgr. Masnovo has tried to prove that by the composition of the *De Unitate Intellectus* Albert played a major part in the struggle against Averroism, although he knew it only in the first stage of its development. Fr. Salman recognises the fact that "the Thomist argument against the Averroistic thesis is substantially the same as that which Albert proposed"; but for purposes of *controversy*, "the argument had to be based on premisses admitted by the adversary", and here St. Thomas shows a definite superiority over his master by taking as the starting point in the discussion the psychological fact *hic homo singularis intelligit*. This distinction seems to be correct; reading Albert's book, one has the impression that he is not completely master of his subject, and that he is not fully aware of the difficulties which are at the basis of the errors of Averroes. From the point of view also of method of procedure, of clarity and vigour of thought, Albert's *De Unitate* does not bear comparison with Thomas's work. One may well agree with Fr. Salman, then, that Albert "played only a secondary part in the philosophical controversy against Latin Averroism.

We have still to speak of Albert's essential work, that which won him an unparalleled reputation in the Middle Ages, and still commands the admiration of present-day historians: namely, his great encyclopaedia of science and philosophy.

Research in literary history has not sufficiently advanced for us to be able to date precisely Albert's Aristotelian paraphrases. But their relative chronology is largely established, and we have already mentioned the arguments against their having been written at Paris before 1248. But we must wait for the decision of specialist studies before opting for a definite chronology. In any case, the question is secondary from our point of view, for it does not affect the general character of his work or its influence on the philosophical movement before the arrival of heterodox Aristotelianism.

What was the part played by Albert the Great in the development of Christian thought ? And what

was the reason for the amazing reputation and remarkable authority he enjoyed even in his lifetime ?
We can see the answers to these questions only if we
bear in mind how far the western world had already
travelled towards its full intellectual development.

We have spoken earlier of the way in which the
first twelve centuries of the Christian era were dominated by the Christian vision of the universe, and how
this state of affairs retarded the progress of profane
science. In the thirteenth century, Aristotle came on
the scene and completely altered the situation; for
the first time, a compact system of scientific and
philosophic disciplines made its way into the Christian
world; theology suddenly found itself faced with
Aristotelianism, the master-piece of Greek thought,
enriched with elements of Arab, Jewish and Greek
neo-Platonism; Christian wisdom was suddenly chal-
lenged by pagan wisdom—profane wisdom, no longer
represented by the modest and inoffensive *cortège* of
the liberal arts, but by the powerful scientific synthesis of peripatetic philosophy.

Conflict between Aristotelianism and Christian
theology was inevitable, since the two views of the
universe differed profoundly on several points. At
Paris, two rival university groups were to come to
blows over it. We have already witnessed the first
skirmish, at the beginning of the thirteenth century.
Theology came off best that time, and its victory
momentarily slowed down the advance of Aristotelianism; but the latter continued to gain ground in
spite of all prohibitions, and March 19th, 1255, saw
the final victory gained. The theologians themselves
could not escape its influence, which went on growing
from William of Auxerre to St. Bonaventure. And it

was just at this point that Albert came onto the scene.

Albert the Great's principal merit does not lie in the fact that he commented on Aristotle; that had been done long before him, at Paris, Oxford, and elsewhere; St. Thomas did it after him, and his literal commentaries are far superior to his master's paraphrases. Nor is his principal merit in the fact that he used Aristotle's philosophy in theological speculation; William of Auvergne and Alexander of Hales had done that quite as much before him. His chief merit rests on this fact: for the first time since the origin of Christianity, *Albert the Great definitely established and clearly defined the rightful position of learning in Christianity*. In doing so, he laid down the principles which could lead to the solution of the formidable problem raised by the introduction of Aristotelianism into the Christian world, and, further, made a decisive contribution to the full development of Christian thought.

It is characteristic of superior minds that they can see through details and accidental circumstances to the clear vision of the real needs of their times. Faced with the new situation created by the full-scale invasion of Greek and Arab learning, Albert realized that the hour had come for Christianity to complete its intellectual emancipation and to take an active part in the scientific movement. Aristotle must be welcomed and his teaching assimilated according to the special genius of Latin and Christian thought; the errors, deviations and lacunae of pagan learning would be more effectively overcome by a constructive effort of reflection and criticism than by prohibition or mutilation of the texts. Following out this fun-

damental intuition, Albert conceived the idea of "re-
making Aristotle for the use of the Latin world";
and for this purpose he undertook the composition of
an encyclopedic work destined to enrich Christian
learning with all the scientific discoveries which the
Greeks and Arabs had accumulated throughout their
history. Fr. Mandonnet writes: "His intention was to
take all the scientific work of which Aristotle was
the principal component, and incorporate into it every
useful element that antiquity, the Arabian masters,
and his own experience could offer. So, gradually,
he formed the idea of a work which would put within
the reach of students the sum total of scientific results acquired by the human mind up to his day" [1].

In order to compose this inventory of the knowledge of his time, Albert did not compose literal commentaries on Aristotle's works as Averroes had done
and as St. Thomas was to do later; no doubt he
thought this method would tie him too closely to
Aristotle's text to suit his purpose. Instead, he followed the example of Avicenna, whose paraphrases had
contributed so largely to the understanding of Aristotle's works. To quote Fr. Mandonnet again: "He

[1] The texts in the prologue to the *Physics* where Albert an-
nounces his great project are well known: "*Intentio nostra in
scientia naturali est satisfacere pro nostra possibilitate fratribus
Ordinis nostri nos rogantibus ex pluribus jam praecedentibus
annis, ut talem librum de physicis eis componeremus, in quo et
scientiam naturalem perfectam haberent, et ex quo libros Aristotelis competenter intelligere possent... Nostra intentio est omnes
dictas partes (physicam, metaphysicam et mathematicam) facere
Latinis intelligibiles...* (Phys., 1. I, tr. I, c. 1. The whole prologue
is worth reading). When Albert began his encyclopaedia, his
brethren had been asking him to do it for many years (*ex pluribus annis*); this is a further indication of its late date.

organized his work according to the general plan of
the latter (Aristotle), but filled it out abundantly
by incorporating material from Aristotle and his
commentators, as well as from his own observation.
This was what made the work such an extraordinary
success—the fact that it provided such an easy guide
to the understanding of Aristotle and put all the
learning of antiquity so conveniently at hand".

The bold stroke of this master in theology was most
significant. Albert's whole manner of action pro-
claimed that the autonomous development of profane
learning was necessary and beneficial, and that theology itself would benefit from it. To this tacit avowal,
he adds the most explicit statements concerning the
specific nature and methods of theology, philosophy
and the particular sciences, based on the data of experience and observation. Albert, then, firmly accepts
the idea of a type of research which in its principles,
methods and internal structure was exclusively rational; he recognizes the lawfulness of a natural
knowledge distinct from supernatural wisdom. His
scientific curiosity is boundless; so varied and so universal is his knowledge that he is at the origin of almost all the doctrinal trends of his century—Thomism, neo-Platonism, German mysticism, and the scientific movement.

Albert's attitude to the assimilation of Aristotle is
a golden mean between the conservative theologians
who are soon to declare open war on Aristotle, and
the members of the Arts Faculty who follow him
blindly even in his most serious errors. With the former, he affirms that faith is superior to reason, that
theology is superior to philosophy, that Aristotle and
the pagan philosophers were sometimes sadly at

fault [1], that the authority of St. Augustine must be respected in theology [2]. But with the latter he recognizes that Aristotle is the most noble personification of philosophical knowledge, that philosophy must be worked out according to its own methods, and that it must be given the benefit of scientific autonomy in the correct sense.

We said a moment ago that Albert the Great laid down the principles which could lead to the solution of the problem raised by the entry of Aristotle. As a matter of fact, his work came ten years too late to *prevent* the development of Aristotelianism in Paris and to stop rationalist Aristotelianism from coming to birth. In fact, his influence contributed to the development of this movement. But the abuse of his ideas obviously does not justify their condemnation; correctly understood, they would have provided a solution to minds which were led astray by too great an attraction for philosophy, enabling them to keep their balance.

Albert the Great is the real founder of Christian

---

[1] He is as independent as St. Bonaventure in his judgment of Aristotle. No doubt he is thinking of Roger Bacon's theory when he writes, concerning the eternity of the world: *"Dicet autem fortasse aliquis nos Aristotelem non intellexisse et ideo non consentire verbis eius... Et ad illum dicimus quod, qui credit Aristotelem fuisse deum, ille debet credere quod nunquam erravit. Si autem credit ipsum esse hominem, tunc procul dubio errare potuit sicut et nos"* (*Phys.*, l. VIII, tr. I, c. 14). In his *Summa Theologica*, Albert expressly condemns Aristotle's errors; cf. M. GRABMANN, *Der Hl. Albert der Grosse*, p. 13.

[2] *"Unde sciendum quod Augustino in his quae sunt de fide et moribus plus quam philosophis credendum est, si dissentiunt"* (II *Sent.*, dist. 13, C, a. 2). *"Dicendum quod sic, quia hoc Augustinus aperte dicit, cui contradicere impium est in his quae tangunt fidem et mores"* (*Sum. Theol.*, II, trac. 14, qu. 84).

Aristotelianism. Some historians have seen in him nothing more than an eclectic, a compiler, whose work, dissipated in unrelated directions, was in marked contrast with the vigorous and original thought of his best pupil, St. Thomas Aquinas. This judgment is extreme. Albert also is a philosopher and a scholar. Throughout his whole life he applied himself to rethinking Aristotle's system, to comparing the tendencies and doctrines of peripatetic philosophy with those of Platonism, neo-Platonism and Christianity, and, finally, to enriching the treasury of learning with the findings of his own research.

However, it must be recognized that he did not arrive at a philosophical synthesis comparable with that of Thomas Aquinas. In his paraphrases of Aristotle, it is difficult to determine to what extent his own opinion is involved—he often remarks that he is merely acting as exegete and does not accept the doctrine he is expounding. Throughout the whole of his work, Aristotle's influence is predominant; but he also gives a sympathetic welcome to neo-Platonic ideas of Greek or Arab origin, while at the same time he accepts the traditional concepts of Latin theology. And all these different strands are not firmly woven into one.

We need not speak here of the resounding success that Albert's work met with in the thirteenth century and up to the end of the Middle Ages, nor of the merits and defects of the vast enterprise, nor of the influence it had on the development of western thought. It is sufficient for our purpose to note that Albert's philosophical works were probably accepted in Paris from about 1255; and that they certainly had a profound influence on the Arts Faculty during the period immediately before the appearance of Siger of Brabant.

### Thomas Aquinas in Paris (1252-1259)

Thomas Aquinas was born at the beginning of 1225, and was twenty-seven years of age when in 1252 he returned from Cologne to Paris to prepare himself for his mastership in theology. He was bachelor in biblical studies from 1252 to 1253, and bachelor in the Sentences from 1253 to 1255. Becoming a master in 1256, he occupied one of the two Dominican chairs from 1256 till 1259, and was then sent to Italy. St. Thomas's first period of teaching was during the time of the conflict between seculars and regulars, in which he took an active part. St. Bonaventure was also teaching in Paris until 1257, and it seems probable that the two theologians met in various circumstances. The period was also marked by St. Thomas's first venture into literature, in which at once we find the expression of his own personal ideas. Among the works belonging to this period are: the *Scriptum super Sententiis* (1253-1257), which closely followed the corresponding work of St. Albert (composed from 1240 to 1242, the definite edition appearing somewhere between 1245 and 1250), and that of St. Bonaventure (1250-1253); the philosophical opuscules *De Principiis Naturae* and *De Ente et Essentia* (about 1256); the *Quaestiones disputatae de Veritate* (1256-1259); the two commentaries on Boethius, *De Trinitate* (1256) and *De Hebdomadibus* (1257-1258); the *Quaestiones quodlibetales* VII to XI (1256-1259); and lastly the *Summa contra Gentiles* (1258-1264).

What were the main characteristics of St. Thomas's attitude towards Aristotelianism ?

He first made contact with Aristotle when he was a student of the liberal arts in Naples, from 1239 to 1244. He was a youngster, barely fifteen years of age when he received lessons from master Martin (of Dacia ?), professor of grammar and logic, and then from master Peter of Ireland, professor in the natural sciences. Later, from 1245 to 1252, he studied for seven years under the direction of Albert the Great and this gave him the chance of broadening and deepening the philosophical knowledge he had acquired in Naples. At the same time, he began his studies in the various branches of theology, using Holy Scripture, the works of the Fathers, the *Sentences* of Peter Lombard, and no doubt other more recent theological works. During this comparatively long period of training, Thomas Aquinas made many reflections, meditations and comparisons, and when we come to read his first writings, we feel we are in the presence of a man who has already chosen the path he is to tread—a man who has already made the fundamental decisions.

Thomas Aquinas made his master's ideas on the autonomy and hierarchy of the sciences his own. In philosophy, he was the first among thirteenth century thinkers to break with the hesitant and wavering attitude of his contemporaries, the first, that is, who firmly adopted the essential intuitions of Aristotelianism, after purging them of later corruptions. Among these fundamental intuitions must be counted especially the theory of knowledge, the doctrine of act and potency, and hylomorphism. In the field of knowledge, St. Thomas definitely opted for Aristotle's

intellectualistic empiricism, rejecting any special illumination at the level of natural consciousness and
any direct intuition of spiritual realities. His theory
of knowledge took as its basis the doctrine of abstraction, to which was added Aristotelian logic. In metaphysics, he adopted the important doctrine of act
and potency which Aristotle had made the key-stone
of his moderate dynamism, but, as we shall see, St.
Thomas brought out the profound metaphysical
signification of this doctrine. In natural philosophy,
he re-established the hylomorphic theory in its authentic form, eliminating all Stoic and neo-Platonic
excrescences which were threatening to stifle it; such
were, for example, *rationes seminales,* spiritual matter, and the plurality of substantial forms.

We should, however, be flying in the face of historical truth if we were to present St. Thomas's philosophy as Aristotelianism pure and simple, or even if we
were to explain it as a preference for Aristotle over
Plato [1]. A quick glance over the Thomistic system is
sufficient for us to see that St. Thomas, following in
this the example of his Arab and Latin predecessors,
borrowed neo-Platonic elements to widen Aristotelianism; his system, like theirs, is a "neo-Platonizing"
Aristotelianism. But his originality and superiority lay
in the rigour of his criticism and in the perfect co-
herence and depth of his philosophical synthesis, in
which Platonic, Aristotelian, neo-Platonic and Christ-

[1] Cf. E. GILSON, *Pourquoi saint Thomas a critiqué saint
Augustin,* pp. 125-126. M. Gilson's expressions would no doubt
be acceptable if they were limited to the domain of knowledge;
but we cannot admit that Plato and Aristotle are "rigorously
antinomic" in their "metaphysics". On the contrary, we think
that St. Thomas's fundamental merit is in seeing their profound
agreement.

ian elements were all given a single, solid foundation. This new philosophy, therefore—*the first really original philosophy produced by the thirteenth century and, even, by Christian civilisation in general*—cannot be given any satisfactory label based on its historical sources. Only one term it apt enough .to express the profoundly personal philosophical attitude of St. Thomas—he created *Thomism*.

Fr. Fabro, writing in 1939, put forward some very interesting suggestions, when trying to establish the ways in which the Angelic Doctor managed to overcome the apparent antagonism between the Platonic and the Aristotelian metaphysics. His idea was that the notion of participation, Platonic in origin, was perfectly harmonized with Aristotle's scheme in the Thomistic system, and was used as the ultimate explanation of the dynamism proper to the system [1]. Fr. Fabro thus provides us with a partly new solution to the problem of the "essence" of Thomism. The role given by Fr. Manser to *the doctrine of act and potency*, and that attributed by M. Meyer to *the idea of order*, is reserved by Fr. Fabro for *the notion of participation* [2]. With a stroke of the pen he silences the most formidable opponents of Thomism, those who see this philosophy as nothing more than an artificial synthesis of Platonism and Aristotelianism. For their theory to be true St. Thomas would have had to place Platonic participation and the empirical naturalism of Aristotle in *juxtaposition*. Fr. Fabro, agreeing in essentials with M. Forest, shows that St.

[1] *La nozione metafisica di partecipazione secondo S. Tomaso d'Aquino*, Milan, 1939; 2nd ed., Turin, 1950.

[2] Of course these points of view are not mutually exclusive, but rather complementary.

Thomas unifies Platonism and Aristotelianism in a higher synthesis, by taking the original step of *transposing* the doctrine of participation. At the level of metaphysical causality, Platonic participation is expressed by St. Thomas's doctrine of the real composition of *esse* and *essentia* in the finite being, and by the total dependence of the finite being on the creative influx of the Infinite Being. The composition of *esse* and *essentia* in turn gives rise to an extension of the Aristotelian notion of act and potency, these notions being used from now on to explain the ontological structure of the composite finite being. All things considered, we can see in Thomism Greek thought rejuvenated and deepened in a highly original way. Fr. Fabro thinks that, as far as the principal sources are concerned, Thomism is a form of Platonism with Aristotelian specifications, rather than the reverse.

These opinions on St. Thomas's metaphysics seem to be quite correct. To realize the depth of the abyss which separates Thomistic from Aristotelian metaphysics, it is sufficient to consider the judgments which each system makes about God and His attributes. Aristotle presents us with *Actus Purus*, which is eternal thought, the supreme cause of movement. For this, St. Thomas substitutes the *Esse Subsistens*, which is the creative cause, the infinitely perfect exemplar and final end of creation, the universal providence that governs the world and calls all created persons to an immortal destiny. Thus, those attributes which are essential to the God of Christianity are discovered at the summit of metaphysics, in the supreme Being, whose existence is affirmed as the metaphysical implication of the reality of which we have experience.

This system of metaphysics has equally remarkable results in psychology and ethics. To keep to the essentials, St. Thomas's solution to the problem of man's nature goes beyond all the suggested solutions recorded earlier in the history of philosophy. He teaches: that the substance of man is one, being a hylomorphic composition; that the soul is spiritual, and is both a substantial and a subsistent form; that in human activity there is a parallel unity and composition, the spiritual element being always in association with the material element in our present state here below. This solid but very subtle doctrine, which corresponds completely with our experience and with the data of our consciousness, has immeasurable repercussions in all departments of psychology, ethics and even theology. But to formulate it in Aristotelian terms, it was necessary to go beyond Aristotelianism itself and to solve the problem of man by referring it to God's metaphysical causality.

St. Thomas's Christian Aristotelianism is therefore a remarkable extension and transfiguration of the peripatetic philosophy, so much so that it becomes a philosophy in its own right, transcending its historical sources. This is not the place to undertake a detailed examination of the doctrinal connections between St. Thomas and his principal sources, nor even to enumerate the various works on the subject. All we intend to do is to make a few observations of general significance.

St. Thomas's attitude towards Aristotle is very aptly described by Fr. Mandonnet when he says that the Dominican master was "the very friendly but independent judge" of the Stagirite. Jules d'Albi's presentation of Thomism as nothing more than a "regression" towards mere Aristotelianism, or as the work of a man blindly infatuated with Aristotle, is a caricature of historical fact. And when Doncœur affirms that St. Thomas "spent his life redirecting or, if you prefer the word, correcting the peripatetic system in order to make it agree with dogma", we can only assume that he just does not appreciate the profound originality of the philosophical aspect of Thomism, or that his mind is not subtle enough to avoid describing, in such ponderous terms, the unobtrusive and often indiscernible influence of Christianity in the development of the philosophical system of St. Thomas.

As for the other pagan philosophers, St. Thomas relies on them even less than he does on Aristotle. It is clear that we cannot put much faith in the over-simplified and exaggerated explanations of such authors as Renan, who says: "Albert owes everything to Avicenna; St. Thomas, as a philosopher, owes almost everything to Averroes".

The problem of the relations between St. Thomas and St. Augustine has been the object of a great deal of fruitful research; but this is not the only problem concerning the Christian sources of Thomistic thought. Many similar problems would merit a detailed examination, for we are still very far from reaching the end of studies into St. Thomas's patristic sources. As regards the sources closest to St. Thomas, the scientific study of the relation between him and his immediate predecessors (Albert, Bonaventure, Alexander of Hales, William of Auvergne and others) has only just begun, and it is possible that quite a few surprises await us. But this research into literary or doctrinal history will not modify the general position of Thomism with regard to earlier or contemporary forms of Aristotelianism. In the near future, we shall probably discover that St. Thomas borrowed freely and sometimes quite literally from his predecessors; from this point of view, historical research tends to diminish the originality of his work. Yet, although he may be to a very large extent tributary of the sources of his material, his own genius is apparent in the philosophical and theological synthesis which he constructs with that material, for to him alone belongs the power of giving life to the synthesis. Considered in the historical perspective of thirteenth century ideas, Thomism emerges as the culmination of all the efforts of arts scholars and speculative theologians to build a new philosophy on an Aristotelian foundation, while taking into account the soundest philosophical conclusions reached since Aristotle, and the essential requirements of Christian thought.

A detailed comparison between the thought of St. Thomas and that of St. Bonaventure would be particularly revealing. It would, we think, show clearly that it is quite wrong to oppose, as two irreducible syntheses, the "philosophy of St. Bonaventure" and that of St. Thomas. On this point the editors of Quaracchi were in the right, as against more recent interpreters of the Seraphic Doctor.

On the philosophical plane, it would be seen that Thomism *amends* the neo-Platonic Aristotelianism of St. Bonaventure, and that by adding depth to the epistemological and metaphysical basis of St. Bonaventure's theology. This explains the corrections made by St. Thomas; the suppression of special illumination and of any intuitive intellectual knowledge; a more critical statement of the problem of God; the substitution of *esse* and *essentia* for spiritual matter and form in the composition of spiritual substances; the return to the authentic hylomorphic doctrine; a more critical attitude towards the problem of the origin of the world in time; the stress on the unity of the composite human being. Exemplarism, which has rightly been seen as the basic principle—indeed the very soul—of St. Bonaventure's system, is a doctrine common to all Christian theology and St. Thomas incorporates it whole and entire into his own system. In metaphysics, it is to be seen in the doctrine of exemplaristic metaphysical causality, while theology uses it in the dogmas of creation and predestination.

On the theological plane, even greater affinities would be discovered between St. Bonaventure and St. Thomas, for both are disciples of the theological tradition of Augustinianism. A philosophical synthesis could not be the final Christian synthesis for either of them; it must be merely a step towards the full synthesis which would be achieved by theology. Theology in its turn is nothing more than the human reflection of the eternal wisdom with which God delights His elect in the Beatific Vision. These opinions are shared by both Doctors of the Church, and it is just as difficult to distinguish between philosophy and theology in St. Thomas's *Summa Theologiae* as it is in St. Bonaventure's *Sentences*.

Therefore, if any attempt is made to find the exact place of each of these two great Doctors in the history of *scientific* progress (that is, in the history of philosophy and theology), it seems impossible to say either that they taught parallel systems of equal value, or that the two systems were essentially different expressions of thirteenth century thought. Of course, St. Thomas's solution to many philosophical and even theological problems differs from that of St. Bonaventure, and we do not by any means intend to force them into agreement by an ill-conceived attempt at harmonisation. But we know from history that these differences are the result of St. Thomas's critical correction of the work of St. Bonaventure, whose strictly scientific activity came to an end in 1257. Thomas Aquinas fully intended to substitute a more vigorous and more coherent philosophical system for the rather neo-Platonic, and still eclectic, Aristotelianism of the Franciscan master. In other words, we are dealing with two *successive* phases of thirteenth century Christian thought, not with two *parallel* forms of it. In the eyes of the historian, the second is an advance on the first.

If anybody wants to discover an *opposition* between the two masters, Franciscan and Dominican, he must move into quite a different domain—that of *Christian life*, or, if it is preferred, of *spirituality*. St. Bonaventure's doctrine admirably represents the Franciscan ideal, which demands a fundamental return to the simplicity of the gospel, a search for God and supernatural values only, a distrust of nature and a contempt for human values. These tendencies appear, especially towards the end of his life, in the judgments he passes on profane learning and philosophy. St. Thomas adopts a more moderate Christian attitude. His ideal of the spiritual life is a harmonious union of nature 'and grace, of what is human and what is divine, of the pursuit of proximate ends and the search for the Sovereign Good. He has therefore a greater desire for philosophical progress and more stringent critical requirements. The differences which we have here underlined are, we think, quite well summed up in the formulae "Christian Extremism" and "Christian Humanism" [1].

It seems probable that St. Thomas's contemporaries did not appreciate his profound originality during the first years of his teaching. With the exception of his first philosophical opuscules, his writings during this period were all theological. His philosophical synthesis was only virtually present in them and it needs careful study to detach it from its context. This is all the more true because St. Thomas did not do anything in too great a hurry, but advanced prudently, avoiding collision with accepted ideas and, above all, with well-established theological traditions.

While St. Thomas was in Paris, the Arts Faculty pub-

---

[1] Fr. Bede LANE, O.F.M., criticised this description of the bent of St. Bonaventure's thought in a note entitled *Christian Extremism* (in *Catholic Survey*, vol. I, n. 1, 1951, pp. 8-10; this was answered by Fr. Nicholas EGAN, O.F.M. (*Christian Extremism*, in *Catholic Survey*, vol. I, n. 2, 1952, pp. 178-181).

M. Gilson and many Franciscan historians with him have well brought out the characteristic traits of this *Christian extremism* in St. Bonaventure's attitude. But, in my opinion, they are wrong in identifying this "Franciscan spirituality" or this "Franciscan ideal" with the so-called "Franciscan philosophy" of St. Bonaventure. They are taking the term "philosophy" in much too wide a sense, as a synonym for *"Weltanschauung"* or "outlook on life". That is the Augustinian sense, but it does not correspond to the use of the word by St. Bonaventure himself, nor to the usage which is commonly accepted today. In the strict sense of the word, we can speak of two antagonistic philosophies only after 1270; it was only then that the conservative theologians, among whom were St. Bonaventure's disciples, set themselves to forging a philosophical system of Augustinian inspiration, in order to keep Thomism in check. This neo-Augustinianism, which later gave rise to Scotism, existed only in germ in the work of St. Bonaventure.

lished its new statutes, dated March 19th, 1255, by which all known works of Aristotle were introduced into the teaching and examination syllabus. Our Dominican master would certainly not remain indifferent to the evolution of ideas among the philosophers of the Arts Faculty, nor would he ignore the growing ascendancy of Aristotelianism over the minds of many. It would be interesting if we could discover in his early writings traces of his concern for the teaching in the Arts Faculty, or some echo of doctrinal controversies which may have been a source of philosophical life in these years. Unfortunately for us, St. Thomas was always sparing with his confidences and rarely indulged in controversies of a personal nature. If, from 1252 to 1259, he had witnessed any openly subversive teaching, he would certainly have reacted against such heretical ideas. But his early works breathe an air of complete serenity. The *Commentary on the Sentences*, the *Commentaries on Boethius*, and the *Quaestiones de Veritate* are an attempt to reconstruct the traditional theology with the aid of a rigorous philosophy, but they do not betray any contemporary philosophical agitation.

Mgr. Masnovo thought he had discovered traces of a reaction against those who taught Arabian or even Averroistic philosophy in Paris, in St. Bonaventure's *Commentary on the Sentences* (1250 ff.) and in St. Thomas's work of the same name (1253 ff.). We agree with Fr. Mandonnet, however, that the texts cited cannot be interpreted in this manner. The words *ut dicunt* could quite well refer to Arab philosophers who had died long ago; the expression *quod si tu dicas* is a common literary usage of the thirteenth century; while the *quidam catholici doctores* who identify God with the active intellect of mankind are theologians who follow William of Auvergne in trying to combine the doctrine of active intellect with the Augustinian theory of illumination. Moreover, the perfect calmness with which both works examine and discuss the errors of Arabian philosophy seems to exclude the possibility of there being in Paris Christian masters who had adopted the heretical ideas of pagan philosophers.

Again, Fr. Gorce thought that he had discovered many indisputable traces of "Latin Averroism" in the *Summa contra Gentiles*, which St. Thomas began in Paris in the spring of 1258, but which he finished in Italy. According to Gorce, all the propositions condemned by the Bishop of Paris in 1270 had already been countered by St. Thomas in the *Summa contra Gentiles*. The word *Gentiles* had "a perfectly well determined meaning in the university", about the middle of the thirteenth century, and although Gorce omitted to give any explicit definition, it is plain from what he had to say about it that he thought the *Gentiles* were the pagan philosophers, Greek or Arab, whose heretical doctrines were being taken up once more by Christian masters in Paris. "There is no need for anyone to believe the Aragonese chronicler, Peter Marsilus (*sic*), who wrote in 1313, that this was a work of Christian apologetic which Raymond of Pennafort had asked for in order to convert the non-Christian subjects of King James of Aragon. It is not very easy to see what profit any but a few doctors or rabbis would gain from a work so scholarly and so difficult in its philosophy". It would be much more readily admitted, continues Gorce, that Thomas Aquinas composed the *Summa contra Gentiles* at the request of Alexander IV, the Pope who, in 1256, had given Albert the Great the task of refuting the error of Averroes in the matter of personal immortality. Thomas Aquinas therefore composed his *Summa* in order to combat the heretical doctrines of the philosophers of Paris.

It is quite true that there is no need for anyone to believe the chronicler Peter Marsilio. But nobody is authorised to reject his testimony without giving any reasons for doing so. Now Fr. Salman, after studying the *Contra Gentiles*, has decisively proved Gorce's theory to be entirely unsupported by the texts. The comparisons which Gorce tries to make between the condemnation of 1270 and the errors combated by St. Thomas in 1258 in no way prove the existence of a heterodox movement at that date. In our opinion, the text of the *Summa contra Gentiles* corroborates Peter Marsilio's testimony, but not in the sense in which Gorce understands it. It is only too clear that St. Thomas's work was not intended to be put into the hands of Moslems, but it was intended for the use of Christian missionaries engaged in the evangelisation of the Moorish peoples. These missionaries had to know something about the philosophical or theological errors which were prevalent among the Moslems, and they had to be armed in such a way as to combat these errors; they had to have some method of preaching which would be suited to the Moslem mentality. This is exactly the situation envisaged by St. Thomas. We need only read the introductory chapters (Book I, chapters 1-9) to find that the *Summa contra Gentiles* is addressed, not to pagans or to Christians who have followed them in their errors, but to the "friends of wisdom", to Christians who respect the Scriptures and are dedicated to the defence of the truth of Catholicism (chapter I). The tone of the work does not seem to be in the least polemical; the author's aim is "to make known the truth which is professed by the Catholic faith and to exclude the errors that are opposed to it". But since the errors of paganism are not always easy to get at, he gives pride of place to the positive exposition of truth, and since the pagans reject the authority of Holy Scripture he prefers to use, as far as possible, the rational method of establishing the truths which are taught by Christianity (chapter 2). The ensuing chapters are also quite obviously addressed to Catholic theologians, who alone are capable of understanding St. Thomas's exposition or even disposed to admit it. The opposition which he proves to exist between the Christian and Mahometan apologetics (chapter 6) also confirms Peter Marsilio's testimony; the thesis on the necessary agreement of revealed truths and natural certitudes is developed without the slightest allusion to any intellectual crisis and without any uneasiness about the relations between faith and reason (chapter 7); and finally, when he is dealing with the method of his work, St. Thomas promises his readers not only apodictic demonstrations capable of convincing un-believers, but also reasons which shall show the suit-ability of the revealed mysteries ("rationes convenien-tiae"); the latter are useful for edifying and consol-ing the faithful, but would be harmful if used against the adversaries of the faith (chapter 9). It is therefore clear that what St. Thomas wrote was a treatise of apologetical theology, for the use of men preparing to preach Christian doctrine among pagans, principal-ly those in Moslem countries.

Of course, Raymond of Pennafort's intervention does not exclude that of Alexander IV. On the contrary, the Pope could have supported Raymond's request with his sovereign authority. Furthermore, even if the *Summa contra Gentiles* was meant primarily for Dominican missionaries charged with the task of converting the Moslems, St. Thomas may still have composed a work of such a scale with the idea that it might be useful to other Christian thinkers also. He was sufficiently aware of the way in which ideas were developing and of the increasing influence of pagan philosophy to perceive how much profit Christian theologians could gain from an exposition of Catholic doctrine which was written with an eye to refuting the main errors of paganism.

We find, then, that neither the *Scriptum super Sententiis* nor the *Summa contra Gentiles* bears any trace of a conflict between St. Thomas and heretics whom he had to oppose. We must therefore conclude, with Fr. Salman, that "we cannot discover any trouble from contemporary heresy in the writings of St. Thomas which date from his first period in Paris. He pays great attention to the Greco-Arabian doctrines, and refutes them with care. But there is no evidence which would allow us to affirm that these doctrines had already been adopted by Latin authors". Fr. Salman continues: "At Paris in 1258, as at Rome in 1256, all they are concerned with is the refutation of "bad foreign books" which run the risk of troubling men's minds. No doubt the real crisis of Latin thought is near at hand, but it has not yet begun".

Not long before leaving for Italy, Thomas Aquinas took part in the General Chapter of the Dominicans, held at Valenciennes on June 1$^{st}$, 1259. Humbert of Romans had called a meeting of the most famous masters, among whom were Albert of Cologne and Peter of Tarentaise, to examine the problem of studies among the Dominicans. The Chapter, being aware of the needs of the day, decreed that each province should in future possess a school of liberal arts.

# CHAPTER VIII

# HETERODOX ARISTOTELIANISM
## (1265-1277)

### Origins of the trend

We have now completed our enquiry into the evolution of Aristotelianism in Paris, and, more generally, into the development of philosophy there since the beginning of the thirteenth century. We are therefore able to fix with great precision the date when the heterodox trend in doctrine, which will be condemned in 1270, appeared. The event must be placed between the years 1260 and 1265. When St. Thomas left Paris in 1259, there was nothing to suggest the approach of a crisis. By 1266, Siger of Brabant had been teaching for a short time in the Arts Faculty, and from 1267 the subversive teaching in that faculty began to provoke a reaction from St. Bonaventure. In the introduction to the *De Unitate Intellectus,* written in 1270, St. Thomas says that the error of Averroes has been gaining ground for some time [1]. All these facts point in the same direction, namely that it is men of Siger's generation who, shortly after 1260, began to teach a philosophy that was frankly heterodox. Of course, this was not a sudden phenomenon, but the result of ideas that had long been

---

[1] *"Inolevit siquidem iam dudum circa intellectum error apud multos, ex dictis Averrois sumens exordium".*

fermenting in men's minds. We have traced the process from before 1250 and there seems no doubt
whatsoever that its progress was accelerated by the
statutes of 1252 and 1255. Yet it was not until 1260
at the earliest that anybody openly professed the
heresies contained in radical Aristotelianism and Arabianism. Moreover, as we have already remarked, it is
unlikely that such teaching could have been propagated for very long without arousing an open reaction on the part of the ecclesiastical authorities.

Circumstances favoured the appearance of this
heterodox trend in Paris. Bonaventure had been
obliged to give up teaching in 1257 and Thomas
Aquinas had gone back to Italy in 1259, with the
result that there was no leading personality left in
the university city. In the theological Faculty, the
best known masters at this time were: Gerard of
Abbeville, who taught from 1255, or perhaps 1252;
Stephen Tempier, the future Bishop of Paris, who took
charge as *magister regens* and Chancellor in 1263,
remaining in this office till 1268; Robert of Sorbon,
master from 1249 or 1250; and the Dominican Peter
of Tarentaise, who occupied his chair from 1259 till
1264. The other teachers of this period have left
hardly any trace. The first years of the new decade
were therefore extremely favourable for the hatching
of heretical doctrines in the Faculty of Arts.

Urban IV, who became Pope in 1261, signed a Bull
at Orvieto, dated January 19th, 1263, in which he
confirmed the privileges, prohibitions and statutes
promulgated in 1231 for the university of Paris by his
predecessor Gregory IX. In this act, which reproduces
*in extenso* Gregory IX's text, the passage concerning
the prohibition of the *libri naturales* (already for-

bidden in 1210) is in no way modified. At once, the question arises as to the meaning of this new censure on Aristotle's writings.

Fr. Mandonnet thought that the reiteration of the decree was a result of the transgression of Gregory IX's commands. But such a reaction would be rather tardy, for Bacon had been teaching from 1240, and the official statute of the Arts Faculty sanctioning the introduction of Aristotle dated from 1255.

Cardinal Ehrle suggested that Urban IV's intervention might be due to the first signs of a developing Averroism. But as we shall see, there were no reactions against Siger and his group before 1267, even in Paris; and moreover, a papal intervention against the young and turbulent school of Siger would not limit itself to the exhumation of a text more than thirty years old, without further comment.

It does not seem necessary to ascribe any particular significance to Urban IV's decree in the history of Aristotelianism. His repetition of Gregory's words can be explained much more simply. The Roman church is conservative, by tradition and by prudence; she does not readily repeal her condemnations and prohibitions, but prefers to let them fall into disuse. Urban IV confirmed the statutes of his predecessor, with all the regulations which they included. To have suppressed any one of them, he would have needed a special reason; he could not think of one himself, and no one else thought of one for him. Why, then, should he revoke a prohibition duly pronounced by the Council of Paris half a century earlier? Moreover, it seems relevant to note that the name of Aristotle does not figure in Gregory's text, and it might well be asked whether the redactors of Urban IV's letter took the trouble  to establish the identity of these *"libri naturales qui in Concilio provinciali ex certa causa prohibiti fuere"*.

What were the main characteristics of the heretical doctrines which were appearing in the university of Paris towards 1260, with Siger of Brabant well to the fore ? We cannot answer the question yet, for the problem can only be solved when we have examined the doctrines and made a study of the reactions they aroused. But we must immediately put the reader on his guard against an idea circulated by Renan first of all, and then taken up by Fr. Mandonnet, that Siger of Brabant was the promoter of a thirteenth century "Latin Averroism". To show how unreliable this opinion is, we need only disclose the method by which it originated.

When Renan undertook the history of the influence of Averroes, he had no difficulty in finding traces of Averroism among the Jews, nor in recalling the really authentic Averroism of John of Jandun in Paris, and that of the school of Padua. But between the death of Averroes in 1198 and the Latin Averroism of the fourteenth century, there was a serious gap; Renan set himself the task of filling this gap by looking for traces of Averroes during the thirteenth century.

Renan fixed the date of Michael Scot's translations at about 1217, and discovered the first certain signs of a reaction against Averroes in the work of William of Auvergne [1]; a page later, we learn that William

[1] "I have only once found the name of the Commentator in his works, but Averroism is refuted on every page, sometimes under the name of Aristotle, at other times under some very vague

was not an adversary but an admirer of the Arab philosopher [1]. According to Renan, then, William refuted the Averroistic doctrines without knowing their origin [2]. The next witness to the struggle against Averroism is Albert the Great's *De Unitate Intellectus contra Averroem*. Renan quotes it according to the text of the *Summa Theologica*, an edition posterior to 1270, and therefore has no difficulty in finding in it the existence of Latin Averroists. Next on the list is St. Thomas, whom Renan takes to be the first disciple of Averroes, because he borrowed from him the method of literal exegesis of Aristotle's works. But he also sees St. Thomas as "the most serious adversary of Averroism", his attack being found mainly in his *Physics* [3] and in the opuscule *De Unitate Intellectus, adversus Averroistas* [4]. This last work certainly does reveal the existence of Latin Averroists. Giles of Rome exposed the errors of Averroes in his treatise *De*

denominations". (E. RENAN, *Averroès et l'Averroïsme*, 4th ed., p.225).

[1] "Thus, in the time of William of Auvergne, Averroes had not yet come to represent the dangerous doctrine of Arabian peripateticism... While Aristotle was energetically opposed and Avicenna was treated as a blasphemer, Averroes was described by William as a *very noble philosopher*, although even then his name was beginning to be abused and inconsiderate disciples were distorting his opinions" (*ibid.*, p. 226-227).

[2] In actual fact, it is not Averroism but Avicennianism that is "refuted on every page" by William of Auvergne.

[3] "The commentary on the VIII[th] book of the Physics is given over almost entirely to a refutation of the commentary of Averroes" (*ibid.*, p. 238).

[4] *Ibidem*, p. 239, where Renan declares: "Opuscule XXVII, *De Aeternitate Mundi, contra murmurantes*, seems to be directed against the same adversaries". Apparently he did not take the trouble to read it.

*Erroribus Philosophorum,* and refuted them in several other writings. Finally, Raymond Lull led a veritable crusade against Averroism.

From this rapid inquiry, which revealed to him the existence of a reaction against Averroism in the thirteenth century, Renan concluded that a school of Averroism must have existed, so he set himself to finding traces of it. He was rewarded by the discovery of two centres of Averroism in the thirteenth century, namely the Franciscan school and the university of Paris. In the case of the Franciscan school, Renan committed a real schoolboy howler; this was due to the fact that in all his work he constantly confused two Arabian doctrines which are fundamentally different both in their meaning and in their effects on the religious and moral order. The doctrines are the unicity of the *active* intellect, and the unicity of the *possible* intellect. Only the second of these is characteristic of heterodox Averroism, for it destroys the moral order by suppressing the fact of a future life and of individual sanctions in the next world[1]. The Franciscan masters followed William of Auvergne in upholding the thesis that there is one unique *active* intellect, which they identified with God, but not one of them subscribed to the Averroistic heresy which taught the unicity of the *possible* intellect. As for the university of Paris, it was in the Arts Faculty that Averroism could be found, according to Renan. He thought that the thirteen propositions condemned in 1270 (Renan mistakenly wrote 1269) by the Bishop of Paris were for the most part "nothing but familiar

[1] It is curious to find that the same confusion as Renan makes is to be seen in many contemporary historians, even important ones, such as Gilson, Geyer, Glorieux, etc.

axioms of Averroism". He recalled William of Tocco's witness to the existence of Averroism in Paris, and suspected that the "Siger" who wrote the *De Anima Intellectiva* and who was glorified by Dante might be one of the masters whom St. Thomas had in mind when writing his *De Unitate Intellectus contra Averroistas*. Lastly, he showed that the great condemnation of 1277 was conclusive evidence that there was in the Arts Faculty of Paris a rationalist trend, according to which the philosophical order and the theological order were radically opposed.

A short criticism of Renan's account enables us to reduce his certain conclusions to the following points. The great scholastics from William of Auvergne onwards knew of the works of Averroes. They criticised the doctrine of the eternity of the world, a thesis common to the whole peripatetic school. The specifically Averroistic doctrine of the unity of the possible intellect was seen to involve disastrous consequences, and was condemned and refuted at least from Albert the Great onwards. Towards 1270, some Parisian masters returned to this fatal error of Averroes and for this reason are called *Averroistae*. Finally, the 1277 condemnation and the writings of Raymond Lull show that a rationalist mentality was to be found among these "Averroists"; this mentality accentuated the opposition between philosophy and theology, and was not unlike Averroes's own attitude to the problem of the relations between reason and religion. In short, the Latin Averroism which Renan showed to exist in the thirteenth century can be reduced to the doctrine of the possible intellect taught by some masters of Paris in the second half of the century, and to a rationalist outlook which may have been inspired by Averroes.

For further knowledge about the importance of this Latin Averroism, we should have to study not only the writings of the masters condemned in 1270 and 1277, but also the texts of the condemnations themselves. An attempt would also have to be made to determine the nature and origin of the heterodox doctrines to the existence of which these documents bear witness, and to ask ourselves how far they can be ascribed to the influence of Averroes. Fr. Mandonnet, hypnotised by Renan's construction of the history of this period, falls short precisely on this point. He did not realise that in the thirteenth century the term *Averroistae* meant one who was an adherent of heretical monopsychism [1], and that there is no evidence which would allow us to give a wider significance to the term. Right from the beginning of his *Siger de Brabant,* Fr. Mandonnet took it as an established or conceded fact that there was an Averroistic school of philosophy in the thirteenth century, inspired only by Aristotle and Averroes [2]. In the course of the book, he develops and comments on this initial presumption, but it is never called into question, nor properly es-

[1] The term *Averroistae* is used by St. Thomas in his *De Unitate Intellectus* and I do not remember meeting it in any earlier document. It may well have been St. Thomas who introduced it into the Scholastic vocabulary; he gave it the precise sense of "adherent of the monopsychism of Averroes". No thirteenth century text is known to me in which the term *Averroistae* must be understood in a wider sense.

[2] "Side by side with the Alberto-Thomist trend, a trend of pure philosophical Aristotelianism was formed in the second half of the thirteenth century. This owed nothing to anyone but Aristotle and his Arabian commentator, Averroes... In this study we are dealing with this trend, described as Latin Averroism, and with its principal exponent, Siger of Brabant". (P. MANDONNET, *Siger de Brabant,* 2nd ed., vol. I, p. 29).

tablished by a study of Siger's sources or of the exact purport of the condemnations of 1270 and 1277. This omission is even more curious in that Fr. Mandonnet himself edited the *De Erroribus Philosophorum* of Giles of Rome, in which the specific errors of the various pagan philosophers are plainly distinguished.

The theory of "Latin Averroism" owes its success to Fr. Mandonnet, but he himself seems to have sensed the lack of precision in it, for the many comments which he makes on thirteenth century "Latin Averroism" nearly always tend to minimise its difficulties. In the first place, he frequently states that Averroism is above all a *radical Aristotelianism*; then, he recognizes the fact that monopsychism was regarded in the thirteenth century as the chief error of Averroes. He declares that it is not easy to find out what was meant by Averroism in the thirteenth century; he even goes so far as to point out some non-Averroistic sources of the characteristic doctrines contained in the *De Necessitate et Contingentia Causarum*. Finally, he acknowledges the fact that the great condemnation of 1277 was aimed at "peripatetic doctrines in general", but he immediately adds "especially in the form of Averroism, in so far, that is, as it was inconsistent with Christian teaching". This last formulation of the position tends to identify "Averroistic Aristotelianism" with "heterodox Aristotelianism".

All recent historians are under the influence of Fr. Mandonnet, and normally they have adopted his definitions of "Latin Averroism". For instance, Fr. Doncœur, after running through the essential characteristics of the heterodox movement led by Siger, concludes: "To keep to the description we have given, any philosophy is Averroistic which is based on Aristotelianism without taking account of theology or of the philosophical requirements of dogma". The author does not for one moment ask himself if the thirteenth century understood Averroism in this way. Similar definitions of Latin Averroism are to be found in the works of Mgr. Grabmann. Fr. Gorce proposes still wider definitions. He acknowledges the fact that the "tendencies rather improperly called Averroistic go considerably further than the actual thought of the Arab philosopher Averroes", and that "we should be careful to treat as Averroists only those philosophers who put forward the main theses of the Arab Averroes". Nevertheless, he then declares quite suddenly and without any text to support his statement that "in fact, all authors who had some interest in the Jewish-Arab culture of which Averroes had become a sort of symbol were called Averroists". A little further on, we learn that St. Thomas "was a moderate Averroist who spent his time battling against an out-and-out Averroist, Siger of Brabant". The confusion is complete when Gorce, agreeing with L. Rougier, sees Averroism as "the common force of the new heresies". For M. Gilson, "Latin Averroism was, in its very essence, the statement of a factual disagreement between certain philosophical conclusions which were thought to be rationally necessary, and certain doctrines of Christian revelation taken as true on the authority of the word of God". Finally, Mgr. Glorieux joins those who accept Fr. Mandonnet's ideas, and thinks that Siger deserves to be called Averroist because he adopted the whole of Averroes's doctrine.

To illustrate the degree of confusion that exists in the minds of scholars concerning the exact nature of "Latin Averroism", we need only quote a strange passage written in 1913 by an outstanding historian, F. Picavet. It runs: "The recent works of Fr. Mandonnet and M. Gauthier have shown us that an impartial historian can hardly consider the Latin Averroists as the faithful disciples of the famous Moslem philosopher, to whom the orthodox Christian thinkers, such as Albert the Great and St. Thomas, seem infinitely nearer. At an early date and side by side with the real Averroes (that is, the "Commentator" who used doctrines of Plotinus to complete the philosophy of Aristotle), there appears some unbeliever to whom we should attribute all the doctrines hostile to Christianity". So now we discover that Albert and Thomas were "infinitely" more Averroistic than Siger, and "the recent works of Fr. Mandonnet", according to whom Siger was the founder of Latin Averroism, are the origin of this discovery!

The path to be followed is indicated by the mistakes of our predecessors. There are some facts which are certain and reliable; they can be reduced to the following: a *heterodox philosophical trend* existed in Paris between 1260 and 1277; this trend was fundamentally Aristotelian and may be called *radical* or *heterodox Aristotelianism*; when dealing with the intellectual soul, certain of these philosophers accepted the Averroistic interpretation of Aristotle and taught *Averroes's monopsychism*. To get a more precise view of this doctrinal movement, it would be necessary to consult the documents which tell us something of its make-up.

## *The career of Siger of Brabant* [1]

We have no positive information about the place and date of Siger's birth. His name indicates that he was a native of the duchy of Brabant, which, in the thirteenth century, was a fief of the Germanic Empire. His relations with Bernier of Nivelles and John of Huy, his enrolment in the nation of the Picards (one of the four corporations of the Faculty of Arts at Paris), and finally the fact that he was canon of St. Paul at Liège, all suggest that he was born in the Walloon portion of the duchy of Brabant; that is, in that portion in which Romance dialects or dialects akin to French were spoken. As for the date of his birth, we have no reason for placing it before 1240.

Probably when Siger was about fourteen years old (for this was the custom of the time), he went to Paris to study liberal arts. He must have arrived there between 1255 and 1260, and he obtained the mastership six years later, between 1260 and 1265. We may suppose that he was then little more than twenty years of age. His name appears for the first time in the decree of August 27th, 1266, by which the papal legate, Simon of Brion, put an end to the dissensions that had troubled the Faculty of Arts. His first appearance on the historical scene reveals him in the unedifying role of a young and unscrupulous leader, who was determined to impose his views on others by every means in his power.

[1] The following pages on Siger of Brabant are taken, with a few modifications, from an article in *The Modern Schoolman*: F. VAN STEENBERGHEN, *Siger of Brabant* (Vol. XXIX, November 1951, pp. 11-27).

From his very first years as a teacher, Siger professed a disquieting Aristotelianism, without regard
for theology and orthodox Christian doctrine. This is
clear from the *Quaestiones in Tertium de Anima*, the
only work certainly anterior to 1270 that has come
down to us; it is also attested by the reaction of St.
Bonaventure in his *Collationes de Decem Praeceptis*
(conferences given at Paris during the Lent of 1267)
and in his *Collationes de Donis Spiritus Sancti* (Lent
of 1268), as well as by the reaction of St. Thomas in
his opuscule *De Unitate Intellectus* (1270), which
was directed especially against Siger. The young master, however, was not alone in his opinions, for a notable group of masters and students shared his ideas,
as is clear from texts of St. Bonaventure, St. Thomas,
and other contemporary witnesses.

On December 10$^{th}$, 1270, the bishop of Paris, Stephen Tempier, condemned a series of thirteen philosophical errors and excommunicated all who should
teach them knowingly (*qui eos docuerint scienter vel
asseruerint*). The errors condemned may be reduced
to four chief ones: the eternity of the world, the
denial of universal providence, the unicity of the intellectual soul, and psychological determinism.

We do not know what the immediate reaction of
Siger was. If there was a calm, it was of short duration. Public disturbances were but the symptoms of
a profound divergence of ideas on the doctrinal plane.
In the face of the theologians and the orthodox members of the Faculty of Arts, who were led by Alberic
of Rheims, the radical party of Siger maintained an
intransigent attitude of fealty to philosophy and especially to Aristotle, who was for them its incarnation. On the other hand, within the party itself, diver-

gences arose over the interpretation of Aristotle. Some,
among them Siger, came under the influence of St.
Thomas Aquinas and mitigated in some measure their
heterodox position, while others, on the contrary, ob-
stinately persisted in professing doctrines more and
more audacious. Boetius of Dacia, who seems to have
been the principal figure of the group after Siger,
may well have belonged to the extremist wing.

On the side of the theologians and the members
of the Faculty of Arts opposed to radical Aristotelianism, the struggle for the defense of orthodoxy continued after 1270.

Giles of Rome published his little treatise *Errores
Philosophorum* in all probability between 1270 and
1274. This document contains the witness of a contemporary as to how men then regarded the sources
of the heterodox philosophical movement. Between
1272 and 1275 Giles got out another small treatise,
*De Plurificatione Intellectus Possibilis,* in which he
discusses the question of Averroist monopsychism. The
author is visibly impressed by the arguments of the
Commentator, although he gives a solid refutation of
them, a refutation based principally on St. Thomas.

The minister general of the Friars Minor, St. Bonaventure, returned to Paris after the departure of St.
Thomas. During the Eastertide of 1273, in the convent of the Franciscans, he gave an important series
of conferences in which he reacted vigorously against
heterodox Aristotelianism and against the rationalist
tendencies of certain masters of arts in Paris. These
conferences, the *Collationes in Hexaemeron,* were in-
terrupted by the elevation of St. Bonaventure to the
cardinalate. They contain no philosophical refutation
of the errors they denounce; they simply condemn

these errors from the point of view of faith and theology.

Finally, it is doubtless about the same time—that is, between 1272 and 1277—that Giles of Lessines, a Flemish Dominican of the convent of Paris, took the initiative in consulting St. Albert the Great about the new philosophical doctrines that the partisans of Siger continued to propagate. He sent St. Albert at Cologne a list of fifteen propositions that "the most eminent masters teach in the schools of Paris" and that had already been opposed in numerous assemblies, and he begged St. Albert to give the *coup de grâce* to these ill-omened errors. Thirteen of the fifteen propositions coincide literally with the propositions condemned by the bishop of Paris in 1270, to which Giles had added two new articles, one compromising the identity of the body of Christ before and after his death, the other denying all composition in angels and the human soul. St. Albert replied with a small treatise *De Quindecim Problematibus*, a critique of the Parisian philosophers that is mordant in tone, unequal and often obscure in content, and lamentably ill-adapted to the situation. It has all the appearances of the work of an old man (St. Albert was then nearly seventy years of age, perhaps more than seventy) who had spent his forces and was left behind by events.

By a decree of November 23$^{rd}$, 1276, the inquisitor of France, Simon du Val, cited before his tribunal Siger of Brabant, Goswin of la Chapelle, and Bernier of Nivelles. According to the text of the decree, the three masters had at the moment quitted the kingdom of France. It seems that Siger appealed from the tribunal of the inquisitor to the tribunal of the pontifical Curia, which was reputed to be more clement.

Peter of Spain, who had taught logic at Paris about 1240, became Pope on September 8th, 1276, and took the name of John XXI. On January 18th, 1277, warned (probably by the inquisitor) of the menacing situation at Paris, he invited Stephen Tempier to make an enquiry and send him as soon as possible a report on the errors that were propagated at the university. The bishop of Paris was by no means moderation personified. He employed all his zeal in carrying out the order of the Pope and even went beyond the mission entrusted to him. On March 7th, he pronounced on his own authority the condemnation of two hundred and nineteen propositions that expressed the teaching of certain masters of the Faculty of Arts, together with several doctrines taught by St. Thomas Aquinas himself (who had died three years earlier).

This resounding condemnation seems to have put an end to the professorial career of Siger. It is probable that he appeared before the tribunal of the Pope and was declared innocent of the crime of heresy; but he was condemned to a kind of forced stay at the Curia, where he lived in the company of a secretary (a *clericus*). At all events, he died at Orvieto, where the Curia was established under the pontificate of Martin IV (1281-1285); the unfortunate master was stabbed by his *clericus*, who had gone mad. This tragic happening must have occurred before November 10th, 1284, since it is mentioned in a letter of John Peckham, archbishop of Canterbury, bearing that date. It may be noted that Martin IV was the former papal legate Simon of Brion, who had known Siger well at Paris.

## Siger's writings

Up to the present, fourteen certainly authentic works of Siger's have been recovered. They may be grouped in the following way:

I. Aristotelian commentaries. These are the most extensive works of Siger's that we possess. The *Quaestiones in Metaphysicam*, Books I to VII, is the most important work of the master; it was published in 1948 by Fr. Graiff [1]. We have also the *Quaestiones in Physicam* (twenty-two questions on Book II), a *Compendium de Generatione et Corruptione* (a brief literal commentary, unedited), and the *Quaestiones in Tertium de Anima* (seventeen questions on the intellectual soul, unedited).

II. Diverse *opuscula*, which we may class as follows:

On logic: the *Quaestiones Logicales* (three questions are announced, but the first alone is preserved; it is concerned with the signification of universal terms); the *Quaestio utrum haec sit vera: "Homo est animal", nullo homine existente* (the question is answered, in accordance with radical Aristotelianism, by the affirmation of the eternity of the human species); the *Impossibilia* (this is the redaction of six very interesting exercises in sophistry); and finally the *Sophisma "Homo de necessitate est animal"* (a discussion on logical supposition).

On metaphysics: the *Quaestio de Necessitate et Contingentia Causarum* (the author tries to place the necessary and the contingent in the hierarchy of causes); and the *Quaestio de Aeternitate Mundi* (upholding the eternity of all species).

[1] New versions of it have been discovered by Fr. A. Maurer (Toronto).

On physics: the *Quaestiones Naturales* conserved in a manuscript in Paris (two questions—one on the unicity of substantial form, the other on weight); and the *Quaestiones Naturales* conserved in a manuscript in Lisbon (six questions treating of very diverse matters).

On psychology: the *Tractatus de Anima Intellectiva* (in nine chapters Siger treats of the most debated questions touching the human intellect).

On ethics: the *Quaestiones Morales* (five very small questions on themes borrowed from the treatise on the virtues).

Now a few words about the lost writings of Siger. Peter Dubois, who had been a pupil of Siger's at Paris, alludes to questions of his master on the *Politics* of Aristotle and also on the *Libri Naturales*. According to the testimony of the Italian Averroist Agostino Nifo, Siger left a treatise *De Motore Primo*, another *De Intellectu*, and finally a *Liber de Felicitate*. Nifo gives extracts from these works. Certain texts of John Baconthorp seem to indicate a commentary on the *De Anima* distinct from those we now possess. Finally, Siger himself, in the *Quaestiones Logicales*, refers to an earlier work on the nature of the universals and gives the *incipit* of it.

If we except the *Tractatus de Anima Intellectiva* and perhaps the *Compendium de Generatione*, all the writings we know are the direct result of Siger's classwork. Either they are simple *reportationes* (that is, notes taken by students), or they are works drawn up with the help of *reportationes* or of notes which the master had used for his course.

An important disagreement still exists among historians concerning the authenticity of some commentaries on Aristotle. Let us recall the *status quaestionis*. In the manuscript of Munich in which the *Quaestiones in Metaphysicam* is contained, this commentary is preceded by a collection of seven other Aristotelian commentaries: two on the *Physics*, one on the *Meteorologia*, on the *De Generatione*, on the *De Anima*, on the *De Somno et Vigilia*, and on the *De Iuventute et Senectute*. The volume has a table of contents written in the handwriting of the student who copied into his notebook the greater part of the commentaries we have just enumerated and who added other documents also to his collection. In this table, drawn up with remarkable precision, the enumeration of the above-mentioned commentaries is followed by the phrase: *Item, quaestiones super primum, secundum, tertium, quartum et partim super quintum metaphysicorum a magistro Sogero.* The question is whether the words "by master Siger" refer only to the commentary on the *Metaphysics* (this is the opinion of Nardi and Gilson) or to the complete collection (this was the opinion of Grabmann, which I also hold and which is accepted by the majority of historians up to the present).

Mgr. Grabmann based his opinion principally on internal criteria; and after having examined all the commentaries, he concluded that they were "undoubtedly authentic works of Siger of Brabant". To these reasons of internal criticism, I have added an argument based on an examination of the table of contents of the Munich manuscript. But the adversaries of authenticity also based themselves on internal evidence, especially on the doctrine of the *Quaestiones in Libros Tres de Anima*, which I edited in 1931; they argue, further, from the silence of contemporaries and successors of Siger about his "conversion to Thomism".

What are we to think of this divergence of views? I believe, in the present state of the sources, that it is impossible to answer the question definitively. The argument drawn from the table of contents does not have the strictness of a mathematical demonstration. As to the argument from silence brought against the authenticity of the commentary on the *De Anima*, two observations are to be made. First, this commentary in no way implies a "conversion to Thomism" (as certain Italian Danteans have too readily asserted), but simply the abandonment (a hesitant one) of the Averroistic monopsychism. Siger could well have made the step of abandoning that doctrine, a step for which the way had already been prepared in the *De Anima Intellectiva*, without provoking any sensational reactions in Paris. Moreover, all the texts published by M. Nardi (as well as by Fr. Chossat) show clearly that the data on the person, the career, and the condemnation of Siger had rapidly disappeared after 1277. He is not known from the fourteenth century onwards, except by some small treatises put into circulation in the neighbourhood of 1270. His very name is deformed, and curious historical mistakes are made. We should therefore not be surprised if the modification of Siger's theses in his *oral* teaching shortly before 1277 should have left no traces in the Averroists of the fourteenth and fifteenth centuries. Finally the arguments drawn from internal criteria, whether in favour of or against authenticity, are always open to discussion. The certainly authentic writings show a great instability in the thought of the young Brabantine master. He easily changes his views; he seems to be

very susceptible to the influence of his reading and
the criticism levelled against him. Miss Maier notes
judiciously with regard to the problem of weight:
"The mere fact that Siger has hesitated and has not
ceased to seek for new nuances for his doctrine is of
great interest. For this fact makes it probable that
finally, not satisfied with the primitive Averroistic
doctrine, and weary of the ceaseless search for new
modifications, he abandoned it and, following the
example of most of his contemporaries, rallied to the
Aristotelian thesis" [1]. Another example: Fr. Armand
Maurer has recently called attention to a doctrinal
divergence between the *Quaestiones in Metaphysicam*
of Siger and the *Quaestiones in Physicam* published
under Siger's name by M. Delhaye [2]. But it can be
shown that the divergence is more apparent than real,
and that there is a striking parallel between the particular question of the *Physics* and many certainly
authentic writings of Siger (*Impossibilia*, I; *De Anima Intellectiva*, V; *Quaestiones in Metaphysicam*, I,7
and III,8).

In the survey of Siger's doctrine we are going to
give, we do not take into account the works which
are not undoubtedly authentic.

[1] "Le seul fait que Siger a hésité et qu'il n'a cessé de chercher
d'autres nuances à sa doctrine, est déjà d'un grand intérêt, car
il rend tout à fait vraisemblable que finalement, non satisfait
de la doctrine averroïste primitive, et las de chercher sans cesse
de nouvelles modifications, il l'ait complètement abandonnée et
que, à l'exemple de la plupart de ses contemporains, il se soit
rallié à la thèse aristotélicienne" (Anneliese MAIER, "Les com-
mentaires sur la *Physique* d'Aristote attribués à Siger de Brabant", *Revue philosophique de Louvain*, XLVII (1949), p. 350).

[2] Armand MAURER, C.S.B., "Esse and essentia in the Metaphysics of Siger of Brabant", *Mediaeval Studies*, VIII (1946),
p. 85, n. 62.

## Siger's *doctrine*

All present-day historians agree in recognizing a heterodox form of Aristotelianism in the doctrinal current personified by Siger. This heterodox Aristotelianism is the most striking and incontestable characteristic of his school.

When and how did this subversive movement of
ideas begin ? As we have seen, there exists no positive
trace whatsoever of heterodox Aristotelianism prior to
about the year 1265; and it is, moreover, improbable
that a teaching so clearly opposed to the doctrine of
the church could have been given at Paris without
provoking the quick reaction of the theologians and
the church authorities. It seems certain, then, that
about the year 1265 Siger himself—and perhaps together with him, some of his colleagues of the Faculty of Arts— inaugurated a manner of philosophizing that took no account of the exigencies of theology
and of Christian faith.

This daring attitude, however, far from appearing
to the eye of the historian as an unexpected break-
away from a well-established tradition, is looked on
rather as the logical and well-nigh inevitable term of
a long evolution of tendencies that had begun to ma-
nifest themselves in the Faculty of Arts from the
beginning of the century. The arrival of the pagan
philosophical literature led to the discovery of philosophy by the Christian thinkers, and especially by the masters of the Faculty of Arts. The possibility of a purely
rational research and of an autonomous philosophical learning gave the career of these masters an entirely new significance and ten-fold increased interest. On the other hand, the exercise of a philosophical

research based on the study of pagan philosophers could not but throw into relief the many differences of spirit and doctrine that placed the Christian outlook on things in opposition to the naturalism and rationalism of the pagans.

The first crisis came to a head at the beginning of the century, but was quickly overcome by the ecclesiastical interventions of 1210 and 1215. During the course of the following decades, Aristotelianism developed without any notable check; but in the philosophical literature prior to 1250 we have discerned symptoms of a state of mind that could easily become dangerous. The new statutes of 1255 cleared the way for a rapid development of the heterodox tendency in the heart of the Faculty of Arts, while other circumstances also seem to have favoured the growth of this movement at Paris.

We know that Siger was of a fiery temperament, impetuous and easily led into excess. We find in his works that strong and peremptory tone, that pugnacious attitude, that hatred for compromise, which the canon of Brabant manifests in the management of the affairs of the Faculty. On the other hand, Siger was gifted with undeniable intellectual ability; he was a profound thinker, a tried logician, and an assiduous reader of the philosophers; he loved clarity and precision. The few contemporary testimonies that have come down to us show that as a philosopher, he had acquired an enviable reputation. His pupil, Peter Dubois, calls him *praecellentissimus doctor philosophiae* and glories in the fact that Siger was his master; Dubois regards him as a classical author on the same footing as Albert the Great and St. Thomas. A manuscript of the ancient college of the Sorbonne calls

him *Sigerus Magnus,* and Dante places him in paradise
in the company of the twelve sages, by the side of
St. Thomas. And his contemporary Giles of Lessines
testifies in his letter to St. Albert the Great to the
reputation acquired by Siger and his colleagues, *qui
in philosophia maiores reputantur.*

Endowed with such a nature and such talents, the
young master from Brabant seems to have quickly
fallen before the charms of the new movement that
swept through the Faculty of Arts about 1260. He
gave himself body and soul to his philosophical calling
and the study of the great masters. A striking characteristic of his work is its strict and exclusively rational orientation. He had a keen sense of the autonomy of every science in its own domain, and it was
a point of honour with him to quote only from sources that were purely philosophical.

Curiously enough, for Siger and his school this cult
of reason went hand in hand with a cult of tradition,
but tradition of a certain kind. These daring spirits,
who were revolutionary in their outlook and did not
hesitate to ˙overthrow ideas accepted in Christian
circles, professed a veritable cult of *philosophical* tradition. Siger's ambition was not to be an innovator
in philosophy, but to repeat and spread the teaching
of the great philosophers. To philosophize was, for
him, to seek out the thought of the philosophers on
any subject: *"quaerendo intentionem philosophorum
in hoc magis quam veritatem, cum philosophice proce-
damus"* [1]. This strange conception of philosophical research was due to the circumstances in which Western
philosophy developed in the thirteenth century. Con-

---

[1] *De Anima Intellectiva,* VII, ed. Pierre MANDONNET, O.P.,
II, 164.

fronted all at once with the monumental work of
Greco-Arabic science, Latin scholars had to apply
themselves to a very arduous work of assimilation;
and so, for almost a century, practically the whole
of their endeavours was taken up with this work of
exegesis. In the Faculty of Arts, the master of philosophy was one whose essential task was to "read" Aristotle. St. Albert the Great himself was no stranger
to this way of looking at the task of philosophy. In
his paraphrases he often refuses to give his own views
and is prompt to decline responsibility for the doctrines he expresses, declaring that he is performing
merely the task of an exegete [1].

We may summarize the main lines of Siger's philosophy as follows.

His philosophical system is dominated by a theory
of knowledge that is strictly Aristotelian. The doctrine of the universals receives his attention many
times, and he has some interesting views on scientific
methodology and the critique of knowledge. He bases
the absolute value of judgments of the abstract order
on the eternity of the world and all the species.

With regard to the place that metaphysics should
occupy in the system of sciences, Siger shows a hesitation that betrays the latent conflict between the
Aristotelian and the neo-Platonist tendencies that
existed side by side in his thought, as in the thought
of all scholastics. But metaphysical principles mani-

---

[1] See, for instance, the end of his commentaries on the *Metaphysics* and on the *Politics* (ed. BORGNET, VI, 751-52; VIII, 803).
St. Thomas Aquinas reacted against this way of conceiving
philosophical research: "*Studium philosophiae non est ad hoc
quod sciatur quid homines senserint, sed qualiter se habeat veritas rerum*" (*In de Caelo*, I, lect. 22).

festly dominate his entire synthesis, and his meta-physics fully deserved to be called "first philosophy".

There is the same fusion of Aristotelian and neo-Platonist elements in the elaboration of the science of being. The *Metaphysics* of Aristotle is the basic text. The presentation of problems, the framework, the vocabulary, the axioms, and the theses furnished by this work constitute, therefore, the primary materials for the metaphysics of Siger. But in no other branch of philosophy did the disciples of the Philosopher, even the most fervent, depart further from the letter of Peripateticism or more modify its spirit. Sometimes consciously and sometimes unconsciously the medieval commentators of the *Metaphysics* gave Aristotle's ontology a neo-Platonic completion, and this is what we find also in the works of Siger.

The main theses of his metaphysics are these. The principle of all things is the First Being, absolute, eternal, personal, whose existence can be established in different ways. Siger is preoccupied with the problem of the unicity of God, which he solves by way of the doctrine of analogy and participation. The immediate effect of God is unique, necessary, and eternal; it is the first of the separated (that is, immaterial) Intelligences. From this emanate the other Intelligences, the celestial spheres and all the movements of the heavens, and then the world of generation and corruption, all according to the law of eternal necessity. The universe, therefore, proceeds wholly from God, but by a progressive emanation. Creative causality and divine government are communicated by successive degrees and are exercised through intermediaries that become more and more numerous with their ever-increasing distance from the First Source of being.

Creatures are not distinguished from God by a composition of essence and existence, but by their *potentia ad esse* (this meant that, of themselves, they are merely *capable* of existing) and by their analogical and limited participation in the perfection of the First Being. The separated Intelligences are eternal beings, simple, spiritual, unique in their species, movers of the celestial spheres. The last two are the Active Intellect and the Receptive (or Possible) Intellect of humanity.

In psychology, Siger found himself confronted with problems about the nature of the human intellect that Aristotle left unsolved. At the beginning of his career, Siger thought that remaining faithful to the principles of Aristotle and the logic of Peripateticism involved adopting an interpretation similar to that of Averroes: the human individual is a substance composed of matter and a vegetative-sensitive form; but this superior animal is capable of very intimate relations with the Intellectual Soul of the human species, which is a unique spiritual substance composed of two elements, the Active Intellect and the Possible Intellect. The Active Intellect is the active principle of our abstractive thought; the Possible Intellect, its subject. Their activity, since it is exercised in us and by means of our images (*phantasmata*), merits to be called ours and differs in each individual. The will (which pertains similarly to the unique Intellectual Soul and to individuals) is a passive power, actuated by the motives presented to it by the Intellect (here Siger borders on psychological · determinism). Since human individuals are wholly perishable, only the Intellectual Soul is immortal; there are no individual sanctions in a future life, but sanctions are immanent in acts themselves, good or bad, and are realized in the present life.

After 1270, under the influence of St. Thomas's *De Unitate Intellectus*, probably also under the influence of the condemnation of Tempier, Siger modified his position in psychology. In his first reply to St. Thomas, written perhaps before the condemnation, he tried to remain faithful to monopsychism, at the same time answering the objections raised by the *De Unitate Intellectus*. Later, in the *De Anima Intellectiva*, his hesitations became more pronounced; he saw insurmountable difficulties against monopsychism; and he finally adhered to the teachings of the Christian faith.

## Siger's historical role

Contemporary of Albert the Great, St. Bonaventure, Thomas Aquinas, leader of the radical Aristotelians, Siger of Brabant is evidently one of the dominant figures of the thirteenth century. His attitude as a thinker and his doctrinal positions certainly explain many of the reactions of his contemporaries. A knowledge of Siger is indispensable, therefore, if one wishes to fully understand St. Thomas, St. Bonaventure, and in general the thinkers who lived during the last part of the thirteenth century. His historical role was important precisely by reason of the reactions he provoked in all the university circles in Paris.

Siger appears in history as the promoter and defender of philosophy acknowledged and accepted as an autonomous discipline. It is in this role that he took a place in the *Divine Comedy* among the twelve sages who reside in the heaven of light. When Dante and Beatrice arrive at the fourth heaven, that of the sun or light, they find themselves in the presence of a brilliant company of twelve illustrious souls: St. Thomas Aquinas, Albert the Great, Gratian (the great canonist), Peter Lombard, Solomon, Dionysius the Areopagite, Orosius (a disciple of St. Augustine, a historian of paganism, and a Christian apologist), Boethius, St. Isidore of Seville, the Venerable Bede (the three great educators of the West), Richard of St. Victor, and Siger. St. Thomas, who presides over this glorious circle, makes the introductions. Coming to Siger, his immediate neighbour on his left, he says to Dante:

> "This, whence to me returneth thy regard,
> The light is of a spirit unto whom
> In his grave meditations death seemed slow.
> It is the light eternal of Sigier,
> Who, reading lectures in the Street of Straw,
> Did syllogize invidious verities." [1].

These mysterious lines have, all down the centuries, exercised the ingenuity of Dante scholars, and the most curious hypotheses have been put forth. Today it is possible to give a quite satisfactory explanation of Dante's verses.

Dante was convinced that many conflicts arise in this world from the fact that people do not stay within the limits of their job. He was, for example, a fervent partisan of a separation between church and state, between theology and philosophy. The twelve souls who abide in the heaven of light are all men

[1] *Paradise*, X, 133-138 (Longfellow's translation).

who have glorified God by fidelity to their personal calling. Dante had to find someone who would be a personification of philosophy, and who was also a Christian (for he puts no pagan in the heaven of the *Divine Comedy*). Siger of Brabant was his man just because he had fought all his life long for the autonomy of philosophy.

But was not Siger a heretic, combated by St. Bonaventure and St. Thomas, condemned by the bishop of Paris and the Pope ? How could Dante place him in heaven ? This objection gives us the opportunity of stating more precisely Siger's attitude towards the faith. Before the first condemnation (1270), he expounds his philosophical convictions without being anxious about the teaching of faith or theology. After 1270, he becomes disturbed, since the bishop and the theologians have made him conscious of some antinomies between his philosophical thought and Christian teaching. When he defends a heterodox doctrine, he makes a twofold declaration. According to his rule as a philosopher, he only expounds the opinions of Aristotle and the other philosophers; these opinions are false in so far as they contradict the teaching of revelation, which is absolutely true and above every human opinion. So he never tries to escape the difficulty by professing the famous doctrine of the "double truth" (one according to reason, and another according to revelation, the latter possibly contradicting the former). On the contrary, he tries to explain the divergences that appear between philosophical conclusions and revealed truth. One must confess that he never came to a quite satisfactory conciliation; but all historians today agree in admitting that he has always been a sincere believer and that he never was a disguised rationalist, as Mandonnet formerly thought.

Dante, who wrote about twenty years after Siger's death, probably saw the events as follows. Siger had been at one time, it is true, the adversary of St. Thomas and had taught a few dangerous doctrines; but from 1270 onwards he had made serious efforts to avoid heterodoxy and had often professed to be attached to the Catholic faith. From the viewpoint of Dante, the great condemnation of 1277 (which had been criticised at Paris, too, by outstanding theologians such as Godfrey of Fontaines) was the fruit of an envious reaction of conservative theologians (among whom was the bishop himself, Stephen Tempier) against Aristotelianism. St. Thomas had been a victim of the reaction along with Siger. Thus the Brabantine master had become something like a "martyr" of Aristotelianism and autonomous philosophy. The Pope had not condemned him as a heretic, but the hostility of the theologians had led him to a painful exile and a tragic death. In the light of these data, the verses of Dante are easy to understand; St. Thomas does homage to his former colleague of Paris, who had been, just like himself, the victim of his fidelity to Aristotle and to philosophy. The "Street of Straw" was a street in the Latin quarter of Paris in which the schools of the liberal arts were situated; there, master Siger had "syllogized" truths that had provoked the envy of the theologians.

A point on which the accord of historians is not yet fully reached is the precise nature of the heterodox Aristotelianism of which Siger of Brabant was the leader.

In my opinion, an examination of Siger's writings leads to the following conclusions: the capital source of Siger is *Aristotle*; his philosophy is, and intends above all to be, a renascence of Aristotelianism. Besides this principal source, we can discern Proclus, Avicenna, Averroes, Albert the Great, and St. Thomas as secondary sources. The first three represent especially the neo-Platonist influence on Siger's thought; the last two, the Christian influence. To speak of a "Latin Averroism" in order to characterize Siger's philosophy is to contradict the data of history and give a false idea of the philosophical movement of the thirteenth century. Siger's system must be called a *radical* or *heterodox Aristotelianism*.

The reaction against Mandonnet's view, which had become classic many years ago, could not but provoke some resistance among the many scholars who were accustomed to think according to the framework provided by Mandonnet. I was not surprised, therefore, to see some attempts to maintain his position; but these attempts could only strengthen my own conviction. I have already had the opportunity to answer my opponents and refute their arguments [1].

[1] See A. Forest, F. Van Steenberghen, M. de Gandillac, *Le mouvement doctrinal du IXe au XIVe siècle*, in *Histoire de l'Église depuis les Origines jusqu'à nos jours*, vol. 13, pp. 279-283 (Paris, 1951).

An important monograph on Siger has just appeared: J. J. Duin, *La doctrine de la Providence dans les écrits de Siger de Brabant*, Louvain, 1954. In this work will be found hitherto unpublished texts and new details concerning Siger's writings and his philosophy. This work is a valuable confirmation of almost all the opinions I have proposed here.

# CHAPTER IX

# THE GREAT CRISIS
## (1277)

### *The rise of the schools*

We have seen how philosophy penetrated with increasing momentum the Arts Faculty, and even theological circles, during the first half of the thirteenth century. Concretely, this movement became what has been called "the flood-tide of Aristotelianism", and resulted in the formation of a neo-Platonizing "eclectic Aristotelianism"; the latter not very clearly specified, precisely because still rather fluid.

We have seen how, from about 1250, certain dominant personalities appeared in Paris, and much more definite trends of thought developed. Schools grouped themselves round these great masters: Bonaventure and Thomas Aquinas, first in Paris and then in Italy; Albert the Great, particularly in Germany; Siger of Brabant in Paris. The situation grew more complicated. Intellectual life became more intense and more diverse; schools grew up and conflicts broke out between them. The conflicts resulted in the great condemnation of 1277, which we have already spoken of in connexion with Siger of Brabant. But this condemnation had much wider repercussions; it was the pivot on which turned the whole doctrinal history of the period; it was the solution to the crisis which

Aristotle's appearance in Paris had caused. To conclude our enquiry, therefore, it remains for us to put
this event into its context in the history of Latin
Aristotelianism.

As a result of the new statutes of 1255, the Faculty
of Arts was very receptive to philosophical speculation, not only in the domain of logic and ethics, but
also in metaphysics and natural philosophy. Not
much is known of the teaching between 1250 and
1265, but from about that date two divergent
trends appeared: one group of masters followed Siger
of Brabant on his rationalist course, and on several
points professed a *heterodox Aristotelianism*; while
other masters adopted a *moderate Aristotelianism*, and
were respectful of the Christian vision of things.

Siger's party was never more than a minority, probably numbering less than a quarter of the members
of the faculty, masters and students; but he seems
to have won the support of the most striking personalities and the most remarkable thinkers, if we are
to judge by their writings and by contemporary
opinion.

The moderate Aristotelians have remained in
greater obscurity. One may quote two names—Peter
of Auvergne and James of Douai, both of whom are
mentioned in the ordinance of the legate Simon of
Brion, dated May 27th, 1275. The first is famous on
account of his intimacy with Thomas Aquinas; he
was a fervent disciple of his at the time when he was
a professor *in artibus*, and completed his commentaries on the *De Caelo* and on the *Politics*; he is also
himself the author of highly esteemed philosophical
works. James of Douai has been rescued from oblivion
by Mgr. Grabmann; he composed several Aristotelian

commentaries, the most important of which is a commentary on the *De Anima*; the complete edition of this work will no doubt cast new light on the psychological controversies of this period.

There were cleavages in the Faculty of Theology just as much as in the Arts Faculty; though here the divergences were of a different kind. We know that from about 1220 Aristotelianism had begun to develop in the Faculty, and had fused with the traditional theological doctrines. In this way, a relatively coherent body of doctrine grew up; between 1250 and 1257 it was taken over by St. Bonaventure and set on a solid foundation. This neo-Platonic Aristotelianism, still fairly eclectic, had become the common philosophy of most theologians in Paris, especially the seculars and Franciscans. Then, in January, 1269, Thomas Aquinas returned from Italy and resumed direction of the Dominican school. His philosophical thought had been distinctive enough when he left Paris ten years earlier, and in the meantime it had reached full maturity. In many points both his theology and his philosophy deviated from the teaching which had become traditional to the Paris theologians. What was more serious still, his Aristotelianism, purer and more critical than that of the other theologians, brought him closer to Siger of Brabant on many subjects. In the eyes of conservative theologians, St. Thomas was to appear as the ally, later as the accomplice, of heterodox Aristotelians.

Such was the situation as the year 1270 approached; it was, then, inevitable that conflict should break out among the various groups just described.

## Doctrinal conflicts

From 1267, the theologians took up arms against
Siger's party. On three occasions, each time in more
explicit and more violent terms, the Franciscan minister general, St. Bonaventure, denounced a new paganism which threatened Christianity, through the
naturalism and rationalism of a good many Parisian
masters. The *Collationes de Decem Praeceptis* (1267),
and *De donis Spiritus Sancti* (1268) condemned the
most flagrant errors of Siger's adherents, and pointed
to a false conception of philosophic research as the
root cause of the evil. This idea came out more strongly in the *Collationes in Hexaemeron* (1273), in which
the preacher attacked Aristotle directly and said that
his failure to grasp exemplarism was the origin of all
his errors; particularly, he inveighed against the idea
of a separate philosophy, an idea which was unaccept-
able for a Christian thinker, and vindicated the rights
of the sacred science, key-stone of the edifice of
Christian wisdom.

In 1270, Thomas Aquinas entered the lists in his
turn, taking arms against Siger's most pernicious thesis—monopsychism inspired by Averroes. He deli-
berately chose to fight on his adversary's own ground,
that of Aristotelian exegesis and philosophical discussion; and in the resulting work, *De Unitate Intellectus*, staged such a vigorous attack on Siger's positions that the latter was forced to modify his views
in later works.

But it was in this stormy period which began in
1267 that the breach between Thomas and the conservative theologians occurred. In the top rank of these

latter was John Peckham, *magister regens* of the
Franciscan school in Paris from 1269 to 1271. Until
just before 1270, the Dominicans and the Friars Minor
followed parallel paths in doctrinal matters; there is
no trace of philosophical or theological dispute between the two schools before that date, although the
latent rivalry between the two orders must have fos-
tered and indeed sharpened the opposition between
their ideas. But they were united in defence of their
privileges against the seculars, and knew better than
to weaken their position by doctrinal quarrels. As we
have said, the rupture between the two schools was
provoked by the numerous and far-reaching innovations which St. Thomas introduced in his philosophy
and theology. The theologians saw in these innovations dangerous concessions to pagan thought; they
found it intolerable that he should prefer the authority of philosophers to that of saints; he was, in fact,
guilty of culpable complicity with those who were
sapping the foundations of Christian thought by pro-
pagating the heterodox teachings of Aristotle. We
know of two episodes in the conflict between Thomas
and the Franciscan school. The first was at an academic meeting, when he was faced with the assault
of the massed forces of conservative theologians, led
by Peckham, on the question of plurality of forms.
Evidence of the second is to be seen in Thomas's
opuscule *De Aeternitate Mundi* (probably written in
1271); this work contains one of the rare passages
in his literary output where he forsakes his impertur-
bable serenity—he is visibly irritated by the preten-
tion of theologians who dismiss the idea of the eternity of the world as absurd, against the almost un-
animous authority of the great philosophers.

These doctrinal debates continued without remission till 1277; other incidents in the fray have already been noted: the *De Erroribus Philosophorum* and the *De Plurificatione Intellectus Possibilis* by Giles of Rome; the letter which Giles of Lessines sent to Albert the Great, and the latter's reply. One should add to the list the works of Siger and his adherents, as well as the writings of the theologians; and it is probable that other documents of this period will be found sooner or later.

## *The condemnation of March 7th, 1277*

We already know the circumstances which led the bishop of Paris, on March 7th, 1277, to promulgate his thundering decree of condemnation. Although it did not issue from the church's supreme authority and never had more than local reference, this act must be considered the most serious censure of the Middle Ages, and had far-reaching repercussions on the movement of ideas. Stephen Tempier formed a commission of sixteen theologians (among them, Henry of Ghent), and they instituted a hasty and haphazard enquiry. In less than three weeks, suspected writings were rapidly scanned—no doubt each member made himself responsible for a portion of the task; the propositions extracted from these writings were assembled pell-mell, with fine disregard for order, with no effort to systematise or unify them, so that the resulting syllabus of 219 articles abounds in repetitions and even contradictions.

In a prologue to the decree, the bishop castigates the attitude of the members of the Arts Faculty who, under the influence of pagan philosophers, teach the most detestable errors, and then try to escape the charge of heresy by distinguishing between the truth of the Catholic faith and philosophic truth, as if there could be two contradictory truths. He condemns absolutely all the errors enumerated in the following list, and excommunicates all who taught them and all who listened to them, unless they present themselves within seven days to the bishop or his chancellor to receive the punishment proportionate to their crime. Tempier then condemns by name two works, the *De Deo Amoris* (a licentious work by Andrew the Chaplain) and a book on geomancy; with them, he links all works on necromancy, judicial astrology, magic, and, in general, all libels against faith and morals; the same sanctions as above are uttered against the authors and readers of these writings.

Then follows the syllabus itself. Fr. Mandonnet has published the syllabus, and, putting it into logical order, arrives at the following results: there are 179 philosophical errors and 40 theological; the former deal with the nature of philosophy (7), God (25), separate Intelligences (31), the corporeal world (49), man and his spiritual activity (57), miracles (10); the theological errors are concerned with the Christian religion (5), dogmas (15), Christian virtues (13), and the four last things (7).

If we bear in mind the doctrinal history of the thirteenth century and especially the events which fill the years 1267-1277, it is easy to grasp the real import of the act of March 7th, 1277. Since Ehrle's work, it has often been called a reaction of Augustinianism against Aristotelianism. But that is not the

fundamental aspect of the affair. It was a brutal—
and too violent, we shall see—solution to the crisis
which first began to show itself in 1210; the crisis
of the Christian understanding, tottering under the
massive irruption of pagan knowledge. The decree
of 1277 is first of all the reaction of churchmen
against the new menace of paganism; and the reaction
took place in the intellectual capital of Christendom,
because the peril made itself felt more strongly there
than anywhere else. Then, from the university point
of view, the decree represented the Theology Faculty's
stand against the steadily increasing encroachment of
philosophy, and against the increasingly disquieting
doctrinal audacity of the Faculty of Arts. It is certainly true that the conservative theologians and especially the Franciscans claimed the patronage of
St. Augustine and made him their standard-bearer
in the fight against Aristotle; but as M. Gilson observes: "Aristotle's triumph over St. Augustine was
fundamentally nothing else than the revenge which
ancient paganism took on the truth of the Gospel" [1].

But those who claimed to be attacking the errors of
paganism attacked also some of the characteristic theses of St. Thomas (who had died three years previously); Thomism was affected by a series of articles
in Tempier's syllabus, and perfectly orthodox doctrines received the same censure as the worst errors
of Aristotle, Avicenna or Averroes. The Thomist
theses most concerned were those dealing with the
unity of the world, the individuation of spirits and
bodies, the localisation of spiritual substances, and
voluntary operation.

[1] E. GILSON, *La Philosophie au Moyen Age*, p. 540.

Stephen Tempier's intervention crippled the rise of radical Aristotelianism by eliminating the main leaders of the party and forcing their followers into a long period of silence. Did the heterodox movement disappear completely during the next twenty-five years? Or did it continue to smoulder under the ashes until John of Jandun blew it into new flame at the beginning of the fourteenth century, with his open profession of Averroist doctrine ? In the present state of our knowledge no answer can be given.

But the decree was likewise disastrous for Thomism. Tempier's act retarded its progress and gave a new lease of life to that eclectic type of Aristotelianism which St. Thomas had wished to surpass.

In 1277, Latin Aristotelianism was condemned in its two most vigorous forms—that of Siger of Brabant and that of Thomas Aquinas. Thus, at the end of this first period in the history of Latin Aristotelianism, the Philosopher's bid to conquer Christianity seems to have ended in defeat.

In reality, the defeat is only temporary, and Aristotle will end by winning the field. But it is not for us to say how, for our task is finished; the later development of peripatetic philosophy in the western world is outside the scope of this book.

# INDEX OF PROPER NAMES

D/1970/0081/20

Printed in Belgium (1643)
by Nauwelaerts, Louvain